Building Winning Organisations

I0056723

Publishing Details
Building Winning Organisations by Kyle Gimpl
Published by Kyle Gimpl © All rights reserved

The moral right of the author has been asserted. All rights reserved. Without limiting the rights under copyright restricted above, no part of this publication may be reproduced, stored in or introduced into a retrieval system, or transmitted, in any form or by any means (electronic, mechanical, photocopying, recording or otherwise), without the prior written permission of the copyright owner of this book.

1st Edition 2018, paperback.
ISBN: 978-1-925764-10-9

Publishing services by: Publish My Book Online,
www.publishmybookonline.com.au

PUBLISH **MY** BOOK
.ONLINE

Building Winning Organisations

**A complete guide to sustaining
best-in-class performance
for all organisations**

Kyle Gimpl

Contents

PROLOGUE **9**

The Essentials of Winning Organisations 9

Preamble: What Makes a Winning Organisation? 11

THE WINNING ORGANISATION MODEL (WOM) **19**

SIPOC Model 25

EFFECTIVE LEADERSHIP **27**

1. A simple, concise vision defines how the organisation creates value. 32
2. Pursues clarity in communication with all employees and stakeholders 41
3. Engages at every level to ensure the organisation is on track to achieve its critical goals 49
4. Always seeks meaningful data to guide decision-making 52
5. Prioritises time to removing the barriers affecting your employees' ability to work to their full capability. 55
6. Delegates authority to make control decisions to roles close to processes 58
7. Pursues the simplification and improvement of systems 61
8. Actively encourages open, transparent and face-to-face communication 68
9. Positively demonstrates the six core values through their behaviour 69
10. Accepts responsibility for improving the performance wof the team. 83
11. Develops standard work routines. 92
12. Utilises planning processes based on valid data to determine the critical few priority actions .94
13. Assigns clear tasks and regularly reviews progress 97
14. Analyses the degree to which work is executed to the plan. 100
15. Knowledge management systems are owned by senior leadership to develop ASK-LEARN-SHARE behaviour throughout the organisation. 101

VALUE FOCUS **107**

CUSTOMER

16. Specifications for all products and services are clearly defined 111

17. Voice of the customer is incorporated to improve processes via regular formal feedback processes 114

18. Market intelligence and competitor analysis is conducted that considers supply and demand, cost-effectiveness, quality and potential for substitution and business-changing innovation. 117

PLANNING

19. A plan exists that defines how the organisation will ensure that the right people with the right skills are doing the right work in the right way to achieve the vision. .119

20. The degree to which tasks are executed according to plan is measured and a focus for improvement. .122

21. Planning estimates the level of risk (or confidence) of achieving a given performance output 124

22. Planning process includes top down and bottom up verification processes to achieve alignment on the critical tasks required to achieve goals 130

23. No work can proceed without the approval of the budget owner . . .133

24. A financial model built upon process drivers is used to analyse and estimate the value of opportunities. 137

25. The financial model considers the life expectancy for critical assets of the organisation 139

ANALYSING

26. A structured method is established to capture, analyse and improve ideas as input into planning. 141

27. Process simulation is used to understand the impact of interactive variation and bottlenecks when considering high-cost interventions 144

28. Discipline exists for improvement ideas to be subjected to a valid cost-benefit analysis as part of determining priorities 150

ORGANISATIONAL EFFECTIVENESS **151**

LEARNING

29. A "way we work" program delivered by leaders communicates the vision, core values, work routines and role of leaders to employees 155

30. Communities of Practice (CoP) are used to build solutions that are owned within the organisation 156

IMPROVING

31. Goals and objectives are prioritised based upon value. 159

32. No more than five critical tasks at a time are assigned to a person 161

33. Employees have an expectation that they will be held accountable and fairly rewarded for their work. 162

34. Individual performance assessment is always aligned to the overall performance of the team 166

35. The level of effectiveness in finding the right person for the right role at the right time is measured. 171

36. Employee turnover is stable and at a rate less than 10% per year. 173

37. All employees are engaged in seeking to minimise variation, including how work is planned and executed. 175

EXECUTING

38. The organisational design clearly describes how authority and resources are organised to achieve the vision 180

39. Levels of management do not exceed six, with a clear theory explaining the value of the work being done at each level 190

40. The number of direct reports fits within effective limits. 193

41. All employees are given the authority and resources required to efficiently complete their standard work .194

42. All roles have defined: the purpose, authorities, accountabilities, skills, relationship to other roles (vertically and horizontally) and performance outputs 197

43. Customer relationship accountabilities are established in role descriptions. 201

44. Standard jobs are approved within limits by the authorised person. 202

45. Standard work routines for the organisation (including key communication and planning meetings) are established. 203

46. Systems are defined, flowcharted and key roles and accountabilities allocated 205

OPERATIONAL EXCELLENCE **207**

DESIGNING

47. SIPOC Model is understood and applied. 209
48. Management of change is rigorously applied to ensure risk is managed at an acceptable level and improvement will be sustained. 211
49. Organisation invests in research and the application of leading technology in high-value opportunities 212
50. The organisation has access to the expertise required for designing experiments or undertaking complex projects. 216

MEASURING

51. Minimum output measures are run-charted and data guides decision-making 226
52. Process managers understand that control of variation at the input and in-process stages will lead to the least variation in outputs. . . .228
53. Effective systems provide employees with the information needed 229

CONTROLLING

54. It is understood that all variation is waste and it is the process managers role to control variation within acceptable limits 231
55. Process managers utilise cause and effect maps to understand root causes 233
56. Whenever a process intervention is decided the supporting theory is defined and captured 236
57. Process managers understand the impact of cumulative variation in processes 238

APPLYING WOM **239**

List of Essential Characteristics in WOM 245

CONCLUDING COMMENTS **251**

Operational Excellence in safety—My Personal Journey 253

REFERENCES **258**

Prologue

The Essentials of Winning Organisations

I have worked in senior management positions or have assisted senior managers in various organisations for 30 years in applying operational excellence ideas to create a step change in the performance.

Along the way I have been fortunate to learn many theories, learn different ways of doing things and have seen various models or tools applied with varying degrees of effectiveness. I wish I knew then what I know now, as this could have saved a lot of time and effort of many people as they explored ways to improve the performance of their organisation.

The purpose of this book is to provide managers with a model that can be applied to guide organisations to become the best in their class.

The undeniable truth is that we don't know what we don't know. Most organisations have gaps in the way they work that significantly impair how well it functions.

Good people with good intentions often find themselves in senior management positions seeking to be successful within organisations that have many barriers and complexities to overcome. Without a shared knowledge or way of doing things that provides constant focus and guidance, confusion, resistance and collective chaos will affect performance.

New managers often bring a new set of theories or ideas. However, they soon move on and the new flavour of the month comes along. The Winning Organisation Model (WOM) seeks to provide the knowledge of all the essential characteristics that an organisation requires to attain best-in-class performance. It describes the necessary relationship between operational excellence, value focus, organisational effectiveness and effective leadership.

Senior managers must be senior leaders in any winning organisation. In my experience, effective leadership has always been the rate determining factor in the performance improvement of a team.

Gaps in how an organisation functions are often reflected in gaps in the knowledge and behaviours of its leaders. Their underlying motivations and beliefs influence their behaviour.

Gaining alignment in beliefs is essential to aligning behaviour. When a person is asked to behave in a manner that is inconsistent with their beliefs this behaviour will not be sustained or will only be superficially demonstrated. WOM outlines the essential beliefs and practices required—the characteristics that the leaders in an organisation need to establish to achieve best-in-class performance.

The degree of alignment and clarity of the efforts of people to achieve the organisations goals is critical to success. Confusion can be created when introducing new initiatives if there is a poor understanding of how these initiatives contribute to achieving the purpose of the organisation. WOM provides a clear and complete set of characteristics that can be used to assess how well an organisation has connected value focus, operational excellence and organisational effectiveness through effective leadership. WOM provides the clarity of what is required for an organisation to become best in class. By conducting a gap analysis using WOM, the leadership will understand where they need to focus their effort.

WOM provides a complete set of knowledge, beliefs and practices that can be used for gap analysis and improvement. The tips, examples and tools allow an organisation to formulate their own pathway forward that suits their specific circumstances.

Preamble:
What Makes a Winning Organisation?

The purpose of this book is to provide a meaningful outline of the capabilities and characteristics required by any organisation to achieve best-in-class performance. I believe that these essential characteristics are as valid for a corner coffee shop as they are for a sporting team or a global company.

Winning organisations are those that achieve better performance than their peers. WOM draws from real experiences to provide simple, cost effective and valid guidance that can be applied where there may be gaps in understanding, capability or essential characteristics. It is both necessary and efficient to understand holistically how to connect four capabilities:

- Value focus
- Operational excellence
- Effective leadership
- Organisational effectiveness

When organisations are aligned around what they are required to do, they can usually learn how to achieve it. Without alignment, an organisation is unlikely to achieve a winning performance as significant effort is expended pulling in different directions.

 The success of two organisations that are competing for the same customers will be determined by how effectively they create the value sought by the customer. It is always critical to focus resources on high-leverage improvement opportunities. For example, in a fast food service business, data had identified that time waiting to get the food was the major cause of customers going elsewhere. When compared to other improvement ideas such as increasing range of food, improving presentation and improving quality, reducing time waiting was estimated to have the greatest impact on profitability. In this case, the organisation that is perceived by the customer to offer the best delivery time will capture this opportunity.

The rate of improvement for any organisation will impact its long-term success. This is always determined by how effective the leadership is. WOM provides the framework to connect people and processes to improve performance and create value at a faster and cheaper rate.

A theory is valid only while it is useful to define relationships between variables that are supported by the available data. It is central to scientific learning that theories be clearly defined so that they can be tested and where anomalies arise, new theories can be developed to advance learning. For an organisation to thrive, its employees must understand, value and contribute their capabilities to a common objective. Beliefs and theories influence decision-making within any organisation. These should be clearly defined and reviewed as part of organisational development and improvement.

Winning organisations are built from sustained and aligned teamwork from a group of people who can serve their customer better, faster and cheaper than their competition.

A CEO once told me that he saw no need for any fancy improvement initiatives. 'Organisations just need good leaders. Good, strong leaders get things done and make the difference between success and failure,' he argued. When asked to define what makes a good, strong leader and how do we get them, the CEO struggled to provide a clear answer.

Winning organisations do significantly better than their competitors because their people are delivering more of what their customers want more often. They deliver greater value at a faster rate.

They must be dynamic and hungry for improvement. There is a saying that 'if you are not improving you are going backwards'. It is essential to identify and improve in high-leverage areas faster than the competition. This is what matters.

Our world is constantly changing. Every day we see new technology and new ways for people to express themselves. We're more connected than ever, most people have more choice and there is a greater predisposition to immediate feedback. People want instant gratification as they jump from interest to interest. Despite all the change in technology, people's emotional and psychological needs remain the same—a sense of purpose or belonging, a demand for recognition and respect, a desire to be successful (in its many forms) and a desire to be loved.

The wealth of communication options has created broad networks of often shallow communications. Today, people can frequently be seen focusing on their mobile device throughout the day, busy responding to and transmitting brief messages that are more about connection and association than meaningful content.

This short-term focus has become a behavioural norm that seems to be reflected in how organisations operate. Three-year terms for CEOs are becoming the norm. Short-term CEOs often focus on creating a brand to

represent their reign. In response to a reporting timeframe of 100 days or so, the CEO must create the appearance that they have provided increased value for stakeholders. All these modern factors challenge the long-term focus required to create sustainable results.

I recall a discussion with the president of a large resource company. I presented him with data suggesting that the production process was being impaired by a lack of skills and a lack of fundamental knowledge within his workforce. He was quick to agree that there was a problem and asked, 'How long would it take to see the benefits from an effective training program that addressed the gaps?'

'Probably two to three years,' I said.

'I know it is the right thing to do,' he said, 'but that kind of timeframe is too long. My timeframe is this year, so why would I invest in this training?'

Building a winning organisation is a journey that needs to be built upon the right foundations and a sustained focus from the senior leadership. The whole organisation must be clear on what the goals are and clear on the work required to achieve those goals.

As we know from the exercise of asking people to pass a message from person to person down along a line, the final version of the message can often bear little resemblance to the original message. Only when the leadership of an organisation understands the importance of clarity and is truly committed to relentlessly seeking alignment with its people, can they work consistently towards a common purpose.

It has been estimated that 95% of all Lean initiatives fail (http://www.qi-a.com/Hom). I have heard managers say that they are 'Doing Lean' many times. When asked, 'What are the organisational goals?', 'What are the key tasks to achieving the aspirational goals?' or 'How is progress being tracked?' it soon becomes obvious that the clarity and focus is not there.

'Lean' is a philosophy that needs to be understood and applied to improve an organisation's ability to achieve its goals. Without the understanding and commitment required to support this philosophy, it is quite common for the introduction of new terms, like Lean, to confuse or send contradicting signals to the people in the organisation.

For example, if an organisation believes that directing decision-making and budget authority towards senior management will deliver the best results, this belief conflicts with Lean Thinking. Lean requires the delegation of authority and decision-making to the lowest level of competence in the organisation, as this supports the development of faster decision making and better process control.

All businesses need to generate value from their processes, whether they are producing physical products or whether they are delivering services. Providing the context, resources and systems that enable people at the front line to improve processes must be the fundamental priority of a management in pursuit of best-in-class performance.

Winning organisations seek to engage the full capability of those working closest to the processes that produce the products or services that customers pay for. It is the role of management to create the conditions and environment that allows for and motivates its employees to do this in the most effective way.

To engage your employees requires effective communication and values-driven leadership. People are not machines and will react negatively if they perceive they are being treated as such. You can push a button on a machine and it will respond; people are different and need to be treated with respect and dignity to get the best from them. People always have a choice as to how much effort they apply to any given task. If you want them to give their all, it requires leadership that demonstrates to them that they are respected, trusted and will be treated fairly.

Dr Edward Deming, in his studies of the ways of Japanese manufacturing, said, 'The worker is not the problem. The problem is at the top! Management! It is management's job to direct the efforts of all components toward the aim of the system. The first step is clarification: everyone in the organization must understand the aim of the system, and how to direct his efforts toward it.' (https://en.wikipedia.org/wiki/W._Edwards_Deming). It is such an obvious role for management, and yet, it is the area where most managers struggle to deliver.

Today's technology allows for increasing levels of automation to eliminate the variability introduced by people in manufacturing. A modern automobile manufacturing plant is a symphony of robotic technology that can assemble the pieces within tight tolerances.

The use of technology is a critical component of winning organisations. The challenge is to balance the what, when, where and how far to go to achieve the best financial return. If you try to automate a process that is neither well-designed nor controlled, it usually fails. It is always better to define and test theories before investing significant capital in designing a completely new

process or in the optimisation of an existing process. Investment in technology needs to be supported by a business case that outlines clearly how the investment will create the value that justifies the project as a high priority.

Winning organisations embrace change. They invest in learning and to take measured risks with introducing new technology. When the entire organisation understands the key value drivers, they can communicate, learn quickly (top to bottom) and understand how to contribute to creating value for all stakeholders.

The culture in a winning organisation is built upon core values of trust, respect/dignity, fairness, honesty, courage and caring. People work for their own benefit, the benefit of their family and friends, and for the benefit of the organisation. Team and individual goals need to be aligned.

A manager once explained to me, 'It is the role of management to pay the employees the least amount required to get the job done.' This paradigm greatly impedes the ability to build the trust and engagement that is essential for high performance in employees. Winning organisations understand that it is the role of management to achieve the best result for the organisation, the employees and the customers.

In winning organisations, all employees understand that their future prosperity will be determined by how well their organisation performs. The belief that you will be rewarded based on how you and your organisation perform is a motivating one. Only when all employees understand what the organisation's goals are, and what they as individuals and teams need to do to achieve these goals, can their full capability be engaged.

Most organisations today conduct performance reviews. However, these are often ineffective or even counterproductive. Often managers don't understand what they're trying to achieve from the performance system. Often the training is mostly about what is needed to comply with the system rather than how using the system creates value. They don't really understand what they are seeking to create from performance systems. Some leaders may not even accept accountability for the performance of their team members and blame unfair outcomes on the system.

Managers sometimes express their concern about being held accountable for the performance of their team. The argument is that they cannot control how their people work. Once managers accept accountability for their team's work, they become more involved in finding new ways to engage their team collectively and individually.

For example, a manager who is motivated to eliminate all injuries will look at an incident and try and find the best solutions to make sure it doesn't happen again. The motivated manager, in dealing with a slip down the stairs, focuses on actions that ensure all employees are safe when on stairs or ladders. A less-motivated manager will often stop at counselling the individual concerned to 'take more care', as they are motivated to act out of compliance. The difference is their level of care or accountability for the team's performance.

Being exposed to new ideas and new language is generally interesting for people but will rarely translate to the adoption of change unless the context and theory is understood and then applied in the workplace. In performance review systems, the manager is usually motivated to comply with the system, to rate or provide a score and if the employee is lucky, tell the person the outcome in unambiguous terms. When managers understand that the purpose of the performance system is to improve performance, the review becomes more of a discussion between two equals who both desire to improve.

Organisations are built for people by people. Only organisations which can do the following deliver superior results over an extended time:

- Lead people
- Delight their customers
- Tap into that discretionary effort
- Align people to work as a team and focus on the things that matter
- Learn and innovate
- Retain and develop people
- Inspire pride in people to belong
- Be positively viewed regarding core values of care, respect and dignity, fairness, courage, honesty and trust
- Consistently deliver more with less by driving out waste

Winning organisations also feel different and are characterised by a strong sense of belonging, of ownership, of caring for other people, of knowing what needs to be done and for the flexibility that is necessary to adapt and respond to what the organisation needs.

In most cases, people want to contribute their capability and their ideas to produce and deliver quality products and services to someone who appreciates them. People are constantly interpreting, theorising, testing assumptions and learning through asking questions.

Much of this learning can occur in silence (in people's heads). Some of this

occurs in conversation, writing, pictures and through how people behave. These 'people' aspects of organisations must be understood as they are likely to impact the future performance of an organisation.

What people understand and believe, as well as the feedback they receive, will shape how they think and how they behave.

Can you imagine launching a business improvement initiative when the people in that organisation feel they rarely receive clear meaningful task assignments or meaningful feedback on their performance? From my experience, most organisations with over 10 people score poorly on clear task assignment and the provision of quality performance feedback to their employees.

A significant commitment from the leader is required to:

- provide a clear task assignment
- specify clearly what needs to be delivered
- define where one task fits in relation to the priority of other tasks
- develop a sufficiently detailed plan of how a task is to be executed
- define the limits in which resources can be used
- define the authorities that the person can apply in doing the task
- define stakeholders
- define who benefits from doing the task (what is in it for me and what is in it for us)

A winning organisation cannot be successful without making progress in engaging its employees.

Involved and motivated people are the creative capability of the organisation. This is where continuous improvement comes from. Whether you are a large-scale multinational or a small coffee shop, people will make the most difference to your organisation in the long run.

The rate of improvement in any team is always highly dependent on how effective its leadership is. They must demonstrate behaviours that are perceived positively by employees.

Leadership is the key in how successful an organisation will be. The unmistakable truth is, winning organisations need the right people in the right roles at the right time, doing the right work to the right standard.

The leadership must inspire and focus people through their positive values-driven behaviour (core values of care, courage, fairness, honesty, trust and respect for dignity of others).

Communication is a common weakness in many organisations. Leaders often make the mistake of assuming they are good communicators without making sufficient effort to test and ensure that they are communicating as effectively as they might like to assume.

WOM provides organisations with clearly defined characteristics that can be used to identify gaps and opportunities for improvement. The first important consideration is whether the leadership understands, accepts and is motivated to make clear communication, a feature of the organisation. Helping the leadership to accept it is the first step, followed by the desire to make it a strength for the organisation. Success requires discussion and debate, combined with a commitment to act.

The Winning Organisation Model (WOM)

The purpose of this book is to provide leaders of organisations with knowledge that can be applied to create an organisation that will consistently outperform its peers.

I have been exposed to many initiatives, theories, teachings and programs that have contained useful information without ever providing a complete picture. It's a bit like a jigsaw puzzle with some pieces missing and no reference picture to work from. Most managers must learn on the job how to put the jigsaw puzzle together.

WOM is intended to explain all the pieces of the puzzle and how they connect to create best in class organisations. It is the model that I wish I had been provided with at the start of my career. I hope it will assist others in creating better, faster, leaner organisations in the future.

In my experience, when organisations align and focus on a problem, they usually find a solution. WOM seeks to provide clear and essential characteristics that any organisation can quickly use to identify gaps. Most organisations who use WOM will find they already have many of the characteristics at least partially in place.

To be a truly winning organisation requires all the characteristics to be in place and to truly be how the organisation operates. One small error in the process of shooting an arrow at a target can make a big difference in where the arrow ends up, and the same is true of a partial compliance to a characteristic.

Some examples of 'how' to achieve each characteristic are provided in the text. However, the prime objective is to provide a clear understanding of 'what' is required and 'why'. Finding the pathway to 'how' an organisation achieves competency in a characteristic is best determined by the people that make up the organisation.

To achieve the best performance in any field means that you have generated more value than your competitors. Value is determined by the customers or stakeholders, who pay for the products and services you deliver. Customers or stakeholders have limited resources and they must make decisions and choices regarding the allocation of their money or effort.

Customer value can be measured. However, some aspects may be less tangible than others. Sometimes customers themselves may not be able to define why they decided to buy one product over another. Emotions play an important part in your customer's decision-making process.

Winning organisations deliver better value than their competitors. This can be measured by quantity, quality, time, cost, reliability, risk and the emotional benefit the customer receives from being associated with the product.

You must understand the value of the product/s you make, and you must have the processes and people to make those products better than your competition. You must also source and transform the right input materials into the right outputs with the least waste. Employees must be doing the right work in the right way at the right time to ensure that they perform in the way required by each customer. Your employees' effort must always be directed toward improving value.

What your customer wants will change over time. Something that delights them today may be out of fashion tomorrow. Winning organisations require leadership that can connect people to the right information, to see change and manage processes to create better, faster, cheaper, more desirable products.

If your organisation is to improve it must have effective leadership. The purpose of leadership is to improve your organisation's ability to achieve its goals. Leadership must be a key component of manager roles. If a manager has the authority to assign tasks to other employees, then they must have leadership authority and accountability.

It is the work of leadership to create an organisation that:

- Shares common values,
- Is organised,
- Allows people to work to their capability and
- Is motivated to learn and improve.

It is not the leaders job to have all the answers, nor to monopolise decision-making. Effective leaders understand the need for the alignment and engagement of their employees, who will then willingly accept ownership, accountability and control of their work.

The pursuit of clear communications is essential work of leaders.

WOM consists of four key capabilities that must be harnessed to achieve best-in-class performance. The four capabilities are effective leadership, value focus, operational excellence and organisational effectiveness. The Winning Organisational Model describes how effective leadership connects its employees to the right processes to create the most value.

Figure 1: Winning Organisation Model

Effective leadership is a fundamental requirement to becoming a winning organisation. Effective leaders must be competent in value focus, operational excellence and organisational effectiveness. The leadership must understand how the organisation creates value and must listen to signals from its employees and from its processes to focus effort onto the highest value opportunities.

Value focus is about prioritising the effort (or resources) of your organisation to the opportunities that create the highest value. This requires the ability to learn, analyse, plan and execute the right tasks/projects. Understanding the customer/stakeholders' changing expectations, along with competitor or step-change developments must inform and shape your strategies and plans.

Operational excellence involves utilising processes that create value efficiently. These processes should make operations both efficient and effective, which will benefit your customer. Variation and waste is minimised by prioritising what is most important to your customer. A continuous process of measuring and controlling the variability of processes drives achieving the best possible performance. Designing processes that will most efficiently create the value required creates step change improvement.

Organisational effectiveness is having the right people doing the right things in the right way at the right time. The right work is derived from decision-making and the generation of people's ideas to improve performance. The ability to share information, generate ideas for improvement, and innovate comes from the people.

WOM is built upon clarity, which begins with understanding the purpose of your organisation. The purpose defines the underlying value proposition. Decision-making is driven by analysis and validation of value. Value is determined by what customers or stakeholders are prepared to pay for. It is only when customers can exercise discretion that value is truly tested.

Winning organisations develop a clear understanding of value and ensure that their company is creating the most value for their clients.

WOM demonstrates this in the following way:

- Value focus provides the analysis and planning to prioritise where resources are allocated. What, where, when, how and by whom are key outputs defined by value focus. The value is created by changing process performance or design.
- When a person identifies a project, they must first establish the value that project will create and what process the project will improve
- A process measure identifies an improvement opportunity (what). The value of the opportunity is assigned only if it justifies the effort when compared with other opportunities.

The role of effective leadership must provide the clarity, the environment, the organisation and the culture required to continuously refine how your organisation improves. WOM describes in detail the essential characteristics that your leadership needs to develop.

The following capabilities will be discussed in detail:

- Analyse—study cause and effect relationships using data to provide useful predictive theories
- Plan—describe a method or steps that can be followed to achieve a given purpose
- Prioritise—determine the order of things based on a value judgement
- Measure—gather data to describe the performance of something
- Control—be able to determine the result or behaviour of a process
- Design—create a process for transforming inputs into outputs
- Learn—acquire knowledge and skill that can be applied
- Innovate—create new skills that can be applied to achieve a purpose more effectively
- Improve—make better the performance of something
- Execute—put all these things into action

Each of these elements are linked through effective leadership in a consistent cycle of improvement that it is supported by the efforts of aligned and enthusiastic people.

WOM provides a set of clear characteristics to help you achieve each of the four capability areas. Any organisation can assess how well they exhibit each characteristic.

The first component of assessment requires your leadership to evaluate whether they understand the characteristic and whether they want to develop it. It is critical that they're committed to it if it has any chance of becoming a feature of your organisation.

Once the leadership commits to it, the next assessment is how well the characteristic is supported by written materials. Written support can be in the form of policies, standards, systems and work routines. It is only when the people recognise that a characteristic is a feature of how the organisation works that it has been truly implemented.

Leaders often gain valuable insight and learning in completing the WOM evaluation process. For example, a gap in effective planning, may have occurred due to historical reasons that need to be recognised and understood.

No single characteristic is more important than another. As tempting as it may seem, creating an overall score from the evaluation is not the objective. The objective is to identify where there are gaps and to identify, analyse, prioritise, plan and address the critical few areas that offer the greatest value.

This approach, when applied continuously, will result in the fastest rate of improvement toward becoming a winning organisation.

There is no one simple step by step method that should be followed, as every organisation has a different context. The rate of addressing gaps will vary depending on the effectiveness of your leadership and your organisation's environment. It is recommended that once one gap is improved, the next highest value gap should become the priority.

A gap in one area often links to a weakness or gap in another. For example, a leader that does not recognise the importance of effective planning is unlikely to appreciate the importance of measuring how well work is being executed to plan.

A leadership team can quite quickly complete an initial WOM assessment. Knowing where the gaps exist is powerful and can serve to anchor future discussions regarding priority work for the team.

Your organisation must develop all the characteristics before you can become a winning organisation. Effective leadership is often the first area of assessment, as most waste in effort occurs when there are gaps in this area. Discussion of each characteristic is an important opportunity for the leadership team to learn and build clarity around what is required.

SIPOC Model

Winning organisations understand that value is created through transforming inputs into the outputs paid for by customers. SIPOC is a standard model used in mapping processes or in describing steps within those processes.

The SIPOC Model has been used to describe and design processes in Six Sigma and Lean Manufacturing. It first appeared in mainstream businesses as part of the Total Quality Management (TQM) programs that were prominent in the 1980s.

SIPOC stands for Suppliers, Inputs, Process, Outputs, Customer. It can be used to define who, what, where and how value is created from a process.

S I P O C   Model

Supplier → Inputs → Process → Outputs → Customer

Measurement

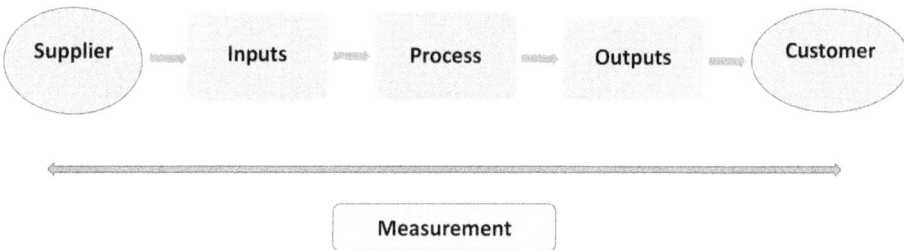

Figure 2: SIPOC Model

The understanding and focus on reducing variation and improving processes is essential to achieving operational excellence. The SIPOC Model provides a framework to describe what needs to be done at each stage of the process.

The **S**upplier provides **I**nputs to the **P**rocess that transforms or transports **O**utputs to a **C**ustomer. To understand and control a process, requires measurement and control actions shared by the supplier and customer.

Operational excellence seeks to maintain the process performance within acceptable limits. Control of variation of inputs and in-process transformation is required to produce outputs that are within specification. Output measures are therefore lagging measures. If the outputs are not within specification, the cause occurred in the input or the transformation (in-process) step. Control measures are required for each stage of any process to enable timely intervention to address variation.

Effective Leadership

1.	A simple, concise vision defines how the organisation creates value
2.	Pursues clarity in communication with all employees and stakeholders
3.	Engages at every level to ensure the organisation is on track to achieve its critical goals
4.	Always seeks meaningful data to guide decision-making
5.	Prioritises time to removing the barriers affecting your employees' ability to work to their full capability
6.	Delegates authority to make control decisions to roles close to processes
7.	Pursues the simplification and improvement of systems
8.	Actively encourages open, transparent and face-to-face communication
9.	Positively demonstrates the six core values through their behaviour
10.	Accepts responsibility for improving the performance of the team
11.	Develops standard work routines
12.	Utilises planning processes based on valid data to determine the critical few priority actions
13.	Assigns clear tasks and regularly reviews progress
14.	Analyses variation in how well work is executed compared to the plan
15.	Knowledge management systems are owned by senior leadership to develop ASK-LEARN-SHARE behaviour throughout the organisation

Figure 3: Winning Organisation Model's effective leadership characteristics are defined

Effective leadership is measured by how well the organisation achieves its purpose over time.

Effective leaders must provide clarity to ensure effort is focused and aligned to create greater value for your customers. The leadership must be invested in improving performance. Competition, changing customer needs, and new knowledge and technology demand that organisations must learn, innovate and improve to remain best in class.

The work of an organisation represents both the intellectual and physical effort. It's important that all employees seek to improve their individual performance and that of the team. The success of any organisation relies on its ability to achieve its purpose. It is the key work of the leadership team to set objectives, develop and focus the capability of the organisation while maintaining risks within acceptable limits.

It is often said that winning organisations look and feel different from other organisations. People who visit or interact with a best in class organisation will often use terms like:

- Efficient
- Well-presented
- Tidy
- Caring
- Quality
- Reliable
- Helpful
- Well-organised
- No one waiting or standing around
- Courteous
- Showed interest in my experience
- Knowledgeable
- Capable
- Proud of their work

This type of organisation does not happen by accident. It requires a level of dedication over time to build and nurture the employees and customers rather than just the bricks-and-mortar elements of the business.

In a winning organisation people are:

- Organised
- Involved
- Able to articulate their goals and objectives clearly
- Able to clearly understand their work
- Follow set work routines and planning processes that allow them to accept ownership of their work
- Clear on their performance and understand how to improve it

- Believe that their performance is important, recognised and fairly rewarded
- Accept accountability as a necessary way of:
  - Clearly defining the work
  - Providing clear authority to do the work
  - Defining what the measurable outputs of the work will be
  - Understanding the value that the work contributes to the organisation and to the individual

People need to be confident in their belief that the leadership of their organisation are trustworthy, honest, caring and fair. They must believe that their leaders respect the dignity of others and have the courage to hold yourselves accountable to a high standard.

Your organisation should be driven by the 'what's right and not who's right' principle. To discover what's right for your customer needs investigation to gain evidence to support decision-making on where to prioritise improvement effort.

There are no shortcuts or magic dust that can plaster over any deficiencies in the leadership of an organisation. It is only when the leadership is united in their desire to improve and are capable of providing the right direction that the important problems can be overcome.

Most organisations can survive without becoming best in class. However, any leader would say they would like their organisation to be the best. Only the organisation with values-driven, effective leadership that is focused on harnessing the abilities of its employees has the chance to win.

For example, if there is high turnover of staff, then deal with that problem before spending effort on teaching people about statistical process control. If there is a low level of trust in your organisation there is no point expecting your employees to take greater ownership of their work.

Your organisation's safety performance provides a clear insight into how well your leadership is doing when it comes to core values and engagement. Few people deliberately seek to be injured in their workplace. It is estimated that in 96% of all workplace injuries, employees knew of the risk and how to prevent the accident occurring.

We know the great innovative and creative aspects of the human brain. We also know that we're is easily distracted, which means people are prone to making mistakes. The only people who don't make mistakes are those who don't do anything (often cynically referred to as managers in dysfunctional organisations)!

While anyone can make mistakes, those who share information and care for each other can create mistake-proof workplaces. For this to occur, the people in the organisation must trust the motives of the leadership. This means leaders must make an effort to build positive relationships with their team. When people care for each other in a workplace, the number of injuries from mistakes is very low. While one person can easily make a mistake, many people rarely make the same mistake at the same time. A caring organisation makes the effort to take appropriate interventions to prevent mistakes that could lead to injury and harm.

Example:

A leading science organisation with a high degree of safety standards and procedures was incurring injuries at a high rate. The incidents were mostly slips and falls. Interestingly, the organisation also had a problem with absenteeism. What could they do?

The senior leader chose to communicate his concerns about safety through email. Most of the line managers considered these types of incidents normal. Hence, they were not their responsibility. After not getting much response to the email, the senior leader decided to begin routine workplace observations to observe, listen to and understand how hazards were being controlled.

The senior leader received an interesting response to his request for area managers to arrange for a suitable time to visit the workplace to talk to the employees about safety. One area manager expressed concern that the senior leader talking to individuals in their workplace would create fear and stress. An alternative approach was suggested—that the senior leader deliver an address to the team, advising them of his concerns about safety at a stand-up meeting.

The senior leader was a friendly person; the opposite to the fearful, domineering manager persona that was being suggested by the area manager. He pushed on with his visits and learnt from the experience, as did the team members, and all the employees clearly appreciated and felt his support to improve.

The most important symbol from this leader's actions was that he cared about safety and he wanted people to take control, look out for each other and in doing so they could count on his support. In going into the workplaces more often, the senior leader also paid more attention to observing how they employees moved around. He noticed many were texting while walking down stairways and running downstairs carrying things. Clearly, these behaviours were causing some of the accidents.

What could be more important than for the senior leader of an organisation to talk to the employees, share and understand perspectives on how they work and what works well, and to explore ways to improve as a team?

There are several key beliefs that the leadership team must understand and demonstrate to be the best it can be. Leadership must be considered as a chain from top to bottom—a break at any point of the chain will undermine the ability to pull in any direction.

The dominant cause of leadership breakdown is misalignment in focus at various levels of the organisation (each level can be viewed as a link in the leadership chain). This is often due to the lack of a shared understanding of the critical issues by each leader.

There are fifteen characteristics that can be used to define effective leadership in WOM and we will explore each in more detail. For each characteristic, there will be a discussion and some short examples to help understand, with supporting theory where necessary.

For each characteristic, there are three questions to answer when assessing the current state of the organisation:

- Does the senior leadership believe that this characteristic is important to their organisation?
- Is there written evidence that supports this?
- Do employees see this characteristic as a feature in how the organisation operates?

There could be many reasons that a leader does not see a characteristic as important but if you want to have a winning organisation, these characteristics are essential. Not everyone wants to be best in class; even so, considering these characteristics is useful in understanding why your organisation is the way it is.

When considering a characteristic some people in the leadership may express different views on whether it exists in the organisation or not. If the leaders express different views regarding a characteristic, this usually means that it is not yet effectively implemented.

1. A simple, concise vision defines how the organisation creates value

An organisation is defined as a group of people who contribute to a common purpose. This purpose defines how effort is focused. Effort that doesn't relate to the purpose results in waste.

Customers must see value in goods or services before they will pay for them. Customers have finite resources and need to make a judgement on whether the benefit justifies the expenditure. For example, many people would like to travel first class. However, only a few are willing to pay for it.

Winning organisations understand how effort translates into value. Understanding value requires analysis and validation.

As organisations grow and more layers of management develop, it becomes more difficult to maintain your focus. It is the critical work of leaders to focus every employee on finding the best ways to move the business forward.

This requires a clear understanding of what your organisation's vision or purpose is and what the measurable goals and objectives are.

Clear Vision

You need to have a simple, concise definition of what your organisation is about so that everyone understands it.

The vision should describe:

- The value your organisation offers to your customer
- How your organisation behaves relative to the wider community
- The inspirational identity you aspire to achieve

The basic premise for any business is that they provide products and/or services to customers. Customers must be willing to pay the amount for the service or products that provides an attractive return on investment.

Stephen Hawking explained that in seeking to expand our understanding of the universe and physics, we must first imagine a possibility and then prove it using mathematics. It is the work of the executive leadership to imagine and test what is possible and then formulate a clear vision and strategy to achieve it.

The executive leadership must be able to anticipate changes in customer choices that will impact their future purchasing decisions. For example, those companies making photographic products that did not see the digital

revolution coming fast enough became largely irrelevant once digital cameras entered the market.

History shows that an organisation's founding strength can often become its greatest blind spot. This can cause the organisation to fail if leaders take it for granted.

History reveals examples of how organisations failed due to blind spots. The Roman Empire dominated the known world for 500 years and was founded upon democracy, values, working together, free debate and its military capability. This was all built upon disciplined organisation and the effective use of technology. However, it failed due to corruption, a loss of morality and the lack of flexibility of the military to respond to what had become more organised and tactically savvy enemies.

It is common for an organisation that has been successful with a strategy to believe that what has worked in the past will work again in the future. It may take too long to develop the new beliefs that are required when the climate around it changes. The beliefs that have contributed most to the success of your organisation will be the most difficult to replace.

A critical capability of senior executives in winning organisations is the ability to imagine and create new possibilities. Senior executives often need to be experienced, have developed technical skills and have proven high analytical skills. A common mistake is to place too high a weighting on experience and technical skill. Creativity, communication, effective leadership are crucial capabilities required by senior executives in winning organisations.

Predicting that a certain individual will be able to create new opportunities may be nearly impossible. However, predicting that a certain individual is unlikely to have the required creative capability is much easier. A CEO who devotes all their effort to short-term urgent work and who is constantly reviewing information generated from the current business environment is most likely not going to create new opportunities. A CEO who invests effort in research and development, who spends time exploring ideas from outside of the current business, and who seeks out emerging new ideas is far more likely to create new opportunities.

Being able to operate existing processes efficiently will not protect your organisation from becoming irrelevant. Imagination and creativity have a habit of coming from the least expected people. At this point in time, people are the only assets that are capable of imagination and creative thought.

The ability to communicate effectively by building new networks can only increase the chance of developing new ideas and innovations. In the end, it is the work of the senior executive to create new opportunities and the executive must value this aspect of their role. They must devote effort to creative thinking and building networks so that they can listen to other creative thinkers.

Example:

An organisation gained enthusiastic senior leader support to launch an operational excellence program.

The CEO engaged his executive team in open communication over several months to gain insight and build ownership of the future direction as a team. The team was united in their resolve to commit to this direction.

However, the president of one division wanted to know how much extra cost should be built into his budget. Another president said that he supported the direction, but that he could not spare any people because the business had some strategic issues that were the priority.

Another was concerned about who was going to do all the work, as he was suffering work overload with the few key people he had.

Despite the apparent support for the idea, there was a clear gap in the planning as to where the new initiative would fit and how it would work.

The critical work of management is to focus on the highest leverage areas. Operational excellence is all about applying scarce resource to these areas to achieve the benefits with least effort. Using a proven system or method can be an effective way to achieve an objective. However, it's fundamental to start with a clear objective.

In some cases, the organisation is simply not stable or mature enough to benefit from trying to do more. If an organisation's leadership cannot truly make change a priority, the right answer may be to wait.

If, for example, the leadership of an organisation is unwilling to delegate control to the lowest level of employee, then a Lean Six Sigma project will likely create confusion and cynicism amongst those employees. Yet this mistake is common.

Managers who say they want their employees to take more initiative are often the ones who are reluctant to delegate authority down the chain of command. Their behaviour demonstrates a lack of trust that is felt and reciprocated by their employees.

It's important to get the underlying thinking right before leaping into action. The vision must provide clarity to your organisation and its objectives. The

starting point is always providing products and/or services to customers at a margin that offers an attractive return on investment.

The starting point is to build clarity around:

- What is our purpose?
- How do we get where we want to be?
- Who is doing what?
- How will we know how we are going?

Whether yours is a new or an established organisation, your first objective should be aligning people's contributions.

A vision is a clear description of what the organisation wants to be. The vision is your identity and purpose, explains where your organisation fits in society. It represents not just what you are offering to your customer, it must also reflect the way your organisation intends to behave in the wider community.

The vision must inspire the right people to want to be part of your organisation and engender a sense of pride in being associated with you.

Vision is the purpose that guides what your team aspires to achieve.

It describes:

- The value you're offering to the customer
- How your organisation behaves, relative to the wider community
- The inspirational identity you aspire to achieve

The vision must be felt through the actions of your employees to make it real.

For a vision to become more than just words on paper, a significant investment must be made by the leadership. What leaders do must be consistent with the vision.

It's important to assess how the leader's behaviour is interpreted by people. He can talk about how important safety is. However, people will observe and make judgements based upon how the leader behaves when there is a conflict between safety and production.

For example, if low cost was a feature of the vision, then the organisation must provide low-cost goods and services. Leaders would be expected to maintain a focus around delivery of the product or service at a low cost.

If a vision only included 'making products at low cost' it would not be very inspirational. It needs to include the social aspect or the personality of your organisation. Where do you fit in society?

A compelling vision needs to emphasise at least one strong societal value. This could be helping people by providing low-cost products or helping the local community by providing affordable services. In this case, the overall motive is helping people. Providing low-cost products and services is how the organisation meets this vision.

One national organisation found that they had a portfolio of businesses spread across the mining, retail, insurance and farming industries. It was difficult for them to define the technical aspect of the vision. They decided that the specific component they were offering was quality management. So, they decided that they had to demonstrate this vision across all branches of their organisation.

A clear and meaningful vision reduces waste as it informs people of overall direction. It provides the necessary context that allows your employees to exercise their discretion for the benefit of your organisation.

Examples of a clear vision:

- World's leading supplier of quality, value-for-money automobiles
- Responsibly providing resources to the world through large-scale, low-cost operations
- Providing services that help the elderly achieve better-than-market buying power

The vision of an organisation provides a clear sense of purpose and acts as filter to screen out areas that it will not consider in its future development. From the vision, a subset of specific tasks or projects must be developed. These will be part of a strategy to move the organisation towards its goal. A plan is required that will move in this direction within a certain timeframe.

An example of this strategy could be:

Vision: World's leading supplier of quality, value-for-money automobiles.

Action: To increase dealerships in major market sectors such as North America and China to capture over 30% of global sales by 2016.

Or.

To ensure that automobile design and manufacturing delivers products that customers desire using purchasing power to ensure the lowest cost.

A vision must describe your value proposition to your customer. Every business exists because it is providing a service or a product that is valued by a customer. The value of this service is determined by what the customer is prepared to pay for it.

In a true customer/supplier relationship, the customer must have the power to choose. When there is only one supply option, the customer has much less opportunity to challenge whether they are getting value for money. Without competition, it is common for suppliers to believe they are improving and doing a good job, while their customers may have a different viewpoint.

Example:

An organisation had been delivering the same analytical service for 15 years to an internal captive customer. Everyone involved in delivering the service believed they were efficient and providing a quality service.

When the service was put into the competitive marketplace, the customer found that they could secure better service at less than half the price they had been paying.

While the supplier organisation was disappointed at losing the customer, they now had a clear challenge to innovate and improve their service for future customers.

It is only when customer/supplier services are tested using data that adequately describes what the customer values that both the customer and the supplier can be confident that efforts to eliminate waste are being focused in the right areas.

The needs and desires of customers are not constant. They often change and sometimes change in ways that the customer themselves wouldn't have predicted. Whoever gives them what they want the most, will be the organisation that they prefer to use.

This requires that they get what they paid for and more. Every customer wants to believe that they have eked out a better deal than everyone else, as this makes them feel successful.

Customers are people and people universally seek confirmation that they have achieved a better outcome than might have been expected from their efforts. Delighting the customer should be your goal if you want a long-term, ongoing relationship. Suppliers that can meet their required specifications and provide some additional value for the same price will be preferred.

For example, if a customer can get the same product at the same price from two suppliers, they will use other factors to determine who he/she uses. This can be as simple as using the company that has nicer employees.

You must have a close understanding of what your customers require. This must go beyond just understanding their specified needs to understanding deeper motivations. This requires considerable effort in building the relationship. You need to gain accurate feedback, and align behaviours and symbols within organisations.

The same core values that apply to people within organisations apply to the people who represent the customer. It is often helpful to consider them as simply the next step in the process or value chain. The end customer always has more freedom of choice than customers within an organisation.

The key attribute of a customer is choice. The customer's choice is influenced by perception, beliefs, observations, information and emotions. Employees are also influenced by these attributes.

Example:

An internal survey of the employees of a large manufacturing company revealed that 70% of them chose to purchase an alternative brand to that made by the company they worked for. What does it say about the product when more than 70% of employees choose an alternative brand?

If you consider that the company offered employees generous price incentives to buy their product this outcome is even more damning. Employees are always either the best or worst advocates for the products or services delivered.

Winning organisations understand that their employees are powerful ambassadors. Effective leaders understand and trust their employees and seek to create an environment where they can confidently and knowledgeably promote the organisation within their community.

When employees feel overwhelmingly positive about the company they work for they will 'go beyond the call of duty' and 'take ownership of the business', freely contributing their discretionary effort.

WOM managers understand that their employees have a choice as to how much effort they apply in the workplace. Employees are customers or stakeholders of the managements work. They observe, interpret, analyse and then draw conclusions that influence their behaviour. All of them have a minimum set of expectations regarding leaders that must be met before they will work to their full capability. If

trust in the product is weak, no manner of incentives will gain their support.

Business Case supporting the vision

Once you have clear process design, customer validation and alignment of the vision, you need to determine whether your opportunity will attract investment. Value is not always about dollars or making more dollars. However, dollars are finite, so finding the most cost-effective way to achieve your goals is always a good idea. Finding the most attractive return from the resources committed requires a valid and compelling business case.

The business case is a valid analysis of the cost, price, volume, risk and margins that suggest that an attractive return on investment (ROI) is likely. An attractive ROI supports the notion that value is being created from the processes proposed.

A simple business model is required that links financial estimates to critical processes and critical tasks to assess value.

The ability to assess all the various ideas and options in a valid, effective and fast manner is required. A financial model describes in a numerical sense what the organisation does and how value or profit is created. Using the SIPOC Model, cost, rates, conversion efficiency, consumption rates of raw input materials, as well as the price of outputs sold, can be estimated to evaluate the profit margin. Even in not for profit (NFP) organisations, nominal values can be used to estimate the amount of value being generated from a process.

Your financial model should project the most likely outcomes expected over the life of your organisation or the process being considered. All organisations should have a view on how long they are likely to be remain in operation. The expected life of the organisation or asset may have a profound impact on how financially attractive certain options will be. Your financial model needs to adequately estimate your costs and the revenue stream. This can simply be based upon profit and loss (P&L) over time.

Your business model must include estimates on the amount and cost of inputs, conversion efficiencies of transformation processes to outputs (including cost of waste) and volume and price estimates for products sold.

It is critical to consider the impact of the uncertainty of the key variables that impact the estimates. As much as one might try to eliminate variation, there will always be some variation. The model should consider the sensitivity to the worst and best outcome and not just the most likely outcome to provide more realistic valuation and to highlight where additional controls might be considered to provide greater certainty.

To achieve the best diagnostic purposes, the model should estimate the impact of variation by incorporating the worst, best and most likely outcomes. If you incorporate key value drivers into the business case model it becomes an effective tool for analysing improvement options or scenarios.

For example, in a chemical manufacturing plant, 70% of the cash costs were associated with the cost of methane gas. The plant uptime and the catalytic efficiency in gas conversion had the most significant impact on the overall cost of the output produced. In this case, the catalytic conversion efficiency was a key value stream for the business. Opportunities to improve catalytic gas conversion, reduce the gas price and keep high plant uptime are likely to improve the return on investment that can be assessed by a suitable model.

It's important to include risk assessment in your business case analysis. Many organisations struggle with this, how can you put a value on safety, for example? I have witnessed numerous occasions where financial decisions on safety or regulatory legislated standards is treated as a separate issue to process improvement investments. This approach can lead to large amounts of money being funnelled into keeping existing processes running without finding the solution with the best return on investment. Using one validated business model for analysis and decision-making will lead to better decisions.

Example:

The structural integrity of an old city building that used to provide health services was assessed. It was estimated that a $500,000 investment was required to restore it to building code standards. But this expenditure would only maintain the building.

In taking a broader look at how to create the most value, they realised that the existing building did not support the services being offered very well. The two-storey building also sat adjacent to an 80-story building which highlighted the value of the land.

When the best value outcomes were considered, best option was to relocate the services to an existing multi-storey building and sell the old property. What would have been a $500k investment became a release of $5 million of cash. The new location provided a more suitable lay out to be provided for the services. The discipline to consider the business case of alternative proposals rather than simply comply to a building standards requirement led to a better value outcome.

2. Pursues clarity in communication with all employees and stakeholders

Where are we going, what do I have to do and how are we going to get there?

These are all important questions that need to be answered before going on any journey. In a winning organisation, everyone knows the answer to these questions. In fact, each person will know how their work fits in with the work of others to create the value required. It is a fundamental component of each leader's work to achieve clarity in all communications.

Achieving clarity does not happen by chance. It requires the ability to put information into context and the ability to interpret, prioritise, provide feedback, question and review, learn and confirm.

Leadership is most effective when it is aligned. Alignment requires organisation and processes.

The pursuit of clarity can be a humbling burden. The leaders of winning organisations know this demands constant effort. Every confused thought or misdirected action is wasted effort and has potential to contribute to further confusion and delays.

Leaders often get the balance between telling and listening wrong. They must understand that their role is to first make sense of all the information and then develop a plan from which clear tasks are assigned. Achieving organisational clarity is never easy. It requires a significant time commitment from leaders to create a culture that is prepared to question and have the courage to seek clarification when necessary.

Example:

The corporate strategy department of a large international organisation announced, after many months of hard work, that its business strategy was complete and the presentation pack for communicating it was available.

As the strategy presentation was rolled out, there were mumblings that the strategy was a bit confusing, a little complicated and not particularly helpful in guiding decision-making. Many were critical of the work.

The strategy document was, however, an accurate reflection of the clarity on strategy that existed at that time. The fact that the senior leadership had made the attempt to put the strategy in writing was a powerful and necessary first step. From this first step further questioning, refinement and discussion was possible.

The attainment of clarity cannot be reached through one-way communication. Effective communication requires a two-way process with as many feedback cycles as are required to achieve the same shared understanding.

Example:

An executive in a large organisation had the courage to ask, 'What is the difference between strategic planning and annual planning?' This sparked a spirited discussion and where it became clear that no one was certain what the difference was. However, from the exchange the team had gained new insights regarding planning processes.

The ability to openly ask these types of questions reflects a positive culture where two-way communication is valued as a necessary part of learning and aligning. In this example, it was safe to question when terminology was unclear. By asking questions, all those involved learn together.

Perhaps the most important motivation in seeking clarity is to answer the question of, 'What do I have to do now that I've received this information?' Feedback loops are activated by questions. Questions such as, 'What do I need to do?', 'How will I know what the intended outcome is?' and 'How will success be measured or described?' and 'Where does this fit with other things?', all help build clarity.

When designing 'failsafe' process control systems, a 'handshake' confirmation is used. The communication is not completed until the recipient sends a confirmation back to the sender to let them know that the message was received and the sender matches the return message to the original message sent.

For important communications people need to adopt similar rigour.

All key tasks must:

- Be written down
- Have clearly defined outcomes
- Be reviewed by the stakeholders
- Be signed off to provide the best chance of alignment and acceptance of the task

Once the importance of clarity is understood and shared and a relationship is established, people can speed up the communication process. By adopting empathetic listening, common language, common routines and recapping steps, people become more in tune and in sync.

It is often only when leaders attempt to write down a key task that they appreciate how difficult it can be to clearly define what you want someone to do.

Communication does not ensure commitment. Often in group situations people assume that messages are either just for information or intended for someone else. When they require commitment, effective leaders demand clarity.

One effective technique in a group setting is to ask each person to signify their commitment to a direction by holding up their hand showing zero through to five fingers. Zero designates no commitment and five signifies 100% commitment.

When there are fewer than five fingers displayed, the leader then asks each person to explain why, asking, 'What would it take for [the person] to move to 100%?' This can be a powerful question.

By creating an environment where open and challenging communication is welcomed by the leader, it is likely that you will achieved a deeper understanding and greater shared commitment to complete the actions. You can feel the emotional energy from a team when each team member offers the full five fingers to reflect their commitment to a direction or action.

A clear and shared understanding may not ensure that the desired outcome will be achieved. However, if there is no clarity at the start it is almost certain that further intervention and waste will occur.

Communication can be defined as:

- The forming of a message
- The sending of the message
- Receiving that message
- Confirmation that a common understanding of the message has been achieved

The Communication Model shown below is useful in helping organisations understand the communication process more effectively.

Communication can break down at any stage so it's important to test for a common understanding. Sometimes leaders assume that because they sent a message, the intended recipient must have received it, understood it, accepted it and committed to act as expected from it.

Communication Model

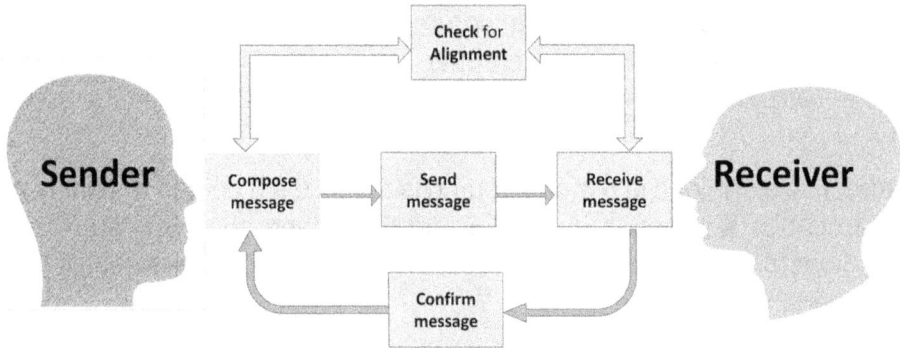

Face-Face is always preferred and written confirmation aids certainty of alignment

Critical behaviour is to seek to understand

Figure 4: Communication Model

Clear communication in the workplace is essential if you want to get the right response every time. However, if you don't get the feedback processes right it is entirely possible that the intended action may fall short of expectations. Feedback systems need data, and not just any data will do. The data must be specific to the purpose.

An organisation sought to improve its overall business performance by implementing an employee performance system to reward people based upon their contribution to the team. What should the feedback measures be? Clear task assignment is only one component.

Consider how to ensure that the tasks assigned relate to the required business outcomes. You need to plan to ensure that these tasks will deliver the required business performance. You need to define a clear purpose. This drives you to think about the measures you require. In this case, to meet the objective of the performance system, you would conclude that the tasks assigned must be derived from the planning process.

Feedback measures need to cover the task itself and whether the plan is delivering the outcomes you require. The performance process must interact with the plan to prioritise tasks and track the progress of task execution and whether the outcomes are in line with what was expected. Feedback allows for adjustment.

The need for planning, task assignment, task execution, progress review and taking corrective actions is generally well understood. Most performance systems fail to effectively incorporate these steps and the required controls to ensure the system meets the purpose for which it was designed.

It is often said that organisations are data rich but knowledge poor. When considering what data to collect it is important to ask, 'Who will use the data?' and 'How will the data be used to improve the process?' The only data that is valuable is the data that is likely to evoke an action if the process moves outside of a determined range.

It must be clear what, when, how and by whom the data will be used. The term data-rich knowledge-poor in an organisation is often symptomatic of a lack of clarity or discipline in considering how that data will be used.

Data is not always information. When organisations collect data that is not frequently used to guide decision making, it often becomes corrupted. Too much data can distract the focus from what is important. Many organisations produce reports weekly, monthly and annually. Often submitting the report on time is more important than what actions have been decided by the manager from the data. For example, an organisation reports monthly the number of work orders outstanding at month end. The report has shown an upward trend for many months, however, there is no corrective action described to reduce the outstanding work orders to an acceptable level. In this example either the outstanding work orders measure is not important, or the management is distracted from actioning the trend.

The purpose of reporting should be to provide the right information to the process manager, so he/she can decide where to allocate resources. Note that a process manager is any role that has the authority to control a process.

Example:

A senior manager in an organisation decided that he would introduce the Pareto Principle into the organisation to in prioritising effort. Pareto is a cause and effect ranking process that highlights the causes that have the greatest impact on an outcome.

Because resources are finite, solving the largest contributing cause before solving lesser causes will, over time, result in a faster rate of improvement than any other strategy. In this example, the manager was interested in reducing the time equipment was out of productive service.

When he saw the Pareto analysis for the first time he said, 'This is rubbish. That data is wrong.' Sometimes this response is enough to derail the use of the data, which makes people simply revert to how things were done before.

On this occasion, the most senior manager announced that since that was the data they had it would be used for decision-making. He added that if the managers were concerned about its accuracy they had better find out how to make it accurate.

The managers quickly established that the major reason the data was corrupted was that it had never been used. Operators had never been taught how to use the data screens and had never had any feedback on their data entry before.

The operators had made a simple decision to acknowledge the prompts generated by the computer as simply and quickly as they could so that they could get on with their job. Once they had been advised of what was required and why, the data was cleaned up and became trusted information to support decision-making.

Eventually, the operators themselves used the information to act in real time. Once they understood what the goals were, they began to act on the data, which greatly improved asset utilisation rates.

Even more important than addressing this opportunity was the improved teamwork and desire to be more involved in further improving performance.

In winning organisations, the senior leadership should always seek feedback to confirm that the purpose or goal will be achieved. The only data that is valuable, clearly relates to the purpose and has clear accountability for action.

Keeping a team or process on track requires leadership behaviour that consistently demands:

- Data that supports a given theory or direction
- Open questioning within the organisation as to cause and effect
- Decisions based upon what is right, not who is right
- Decisions made in a timely manner. Leaders are required to take some risks in decision-making, provided the risks are within acceptable limits. If consensus is the only way decisions are made it is likely that the rate of improvement will be lower than required to sustain competitiveness.

Communication Discussion—the Power of 45 Minutes

Leaders in an organisation were asked to say how often they had had a workplace conversation with an individual in their team that lasted 45 minutes or more. The response was either rarely or never.

To build a meaningful relationship requires a significant investment of time. When leaders do not engage sufficiently with their people this is a missed opportunity to access what each person can offer.

In most organisations, leaders interact with people in a polite and yet superficial manner. Conversation is often limited to a standard greeting, then perhaps the weather and perhaps a few statements or directives. In this style of communication both parties are recognising each other respectfully. However, neither party is expecting anything more. In fact, they're probably thinking more about what they're going to do next than the discussion.

When the conversation continues beyond a few minutes, the progression of topics may drift to sport, general news, etc—safe territory. It might stay there for as long as 15 minutes, during which some rapport could begin to grow. Stopping the conversation at this point will probably leave some mutual recognition that can be built upon in the future.

Continuing the conversation past 15 minutes will bring in elements of how the business is going and exploration of various questions, including family life. At this point people begin to talk about what makes them who they are. Reaching this point in the conversation could be the start of a memorable discussion.

If people sustain communication into that 30–45-minute zone it is common that the discussion will reach deeper beliefs, concerns, aspirations and ideas. This level of communication between leader and team member can provide the common ground from which mutual respect and support can grow.

When conducting safety observations in the workplace many leaders operate only at the superficial level—they observe an act, then provide an assessment and direct feedback based on that observation. But safety is built around the value of care for people. Only when meaningful communication occurs (at some point in discussions beyond 30 minutes) will deeper issues, such as safety concerns, be disclosed. While you may learn something specific after a 45-minute face-to-face conversation, developing a meaningful relationship is even more important, as it will make future connections easier and more effective.

The leadership of a winning organisation must pursue clear communication. This can be demonstrated by:

- People confidently sharing the same understanding of the organisation's objectives
- People having clear tasks and understanding how their work contributes to the organisation's objectives
- Regular scheduled communication sessions involving various levels within the organisation
- Information displayed in the workplace on how the team and the business are performing
- Employees regularly asking questions, sharing learnings and demanding clarity in task assignments and progress on improvement
- Written evidence showing the commitment to clear and common understanding

3. Engages at every level to ensure the organisation is on track to achieve its critical goals

Winning organisations provide better value to the customer than their competitors. Sustaining superior performance requires that you improve faster than anyone else. This is achieved by identifying and executing the right actions or tasks as efficiently as possible.

As resources are always finite, the fastest rate of improvement comes from identifying and executing the opportunities which create the most value and prioritising their completion over lesser value opportunities. The leadership must understand that their most important role is listening, observing, testing and influencing people and the processes to ensure that the organisation is truly focused on the right work.

Leaders regularly go to the workplace to listen, observe and understand how to keep the business on track. Every leader must commit regular and structured time to maintaining focus.

People inherently want to be valued for what they do. They want to be successful. Unfortunately, in many organisations people end up feeling the opposite.

Senior leaders' behaviours must be viewed positively regarding the core values before people will be prepared to give their best every day. Every day, employees interpret what they see and feel through the lens of their beliefs. Employees will ascribe either positive or negative interpretations of their leader's behaviour. What gets attention? How do the leaders make them feel?

It is difficult for a person to fake that they care for others for any length of time; people are quick to realise their true motives. People will judge leaders by what they do, rather than what they say. Only when the leadership's commitment is positively felt by the people can they access the full capability of the workforce.

Every day the leadership needs to consciously reinforce that they value people. This doesn't necessarily require a large time commitment.

Example:

A large smelting operation experienced numerous instances of employees with a lack of respect for each other.

The maintenance department felt that the people operating the plant were careless and uneducated. They were continually blaming people working in operator roles for causing process breakdowns.

Operations people, on the other hand, thought that the maintenance personnel always looked for the easiest option and never returned equipment in a safe and ready manner.

The operations leadership were located at the main entrance to the smelter and maintenance leadership were located at the far back entrance. Maintenance people exclusively accessed their offices from the back, so the two groups were as separate as they could be. The lack of interaction between the two groups helped amplify the negative beliefs each held about the other.

A change was implemented that required all employees to enter through the same front entrance (this was against the wishes of each group's leaders). Daily information and toolbox planning meetings were held, involving all the employees rostered on.

While there were deeply entrenched perceptions between some individuals (particularly between departmental leaders) this simple act gradually contributed to breaking down the 'them and us' attitude. The smelting team began to understand why breakdowns were occurring. Some significant misconceptions between the two groups emerged regarding how equipment was operated which raised questions about whether the equipment was fit for purpose.

Once the barriers to communication were lifted, the team addressed the knowledge, skill and system gaps that were the main cause of the negative beliefs that had formed over the years.

Why would a senior leader not make the effort to recognise an employee and show an interest in the person and his/her work? A simple few words can make that person's day and it takes very little time. Winning organisations require leaders who value and understand their role in creating an engaged workforce.

Winning organisations with effective leadership in this area will demonstrate:

- That leaders regularly interact with their employees
- That they are producing written information on the progress of both the team and the organisation. This information will be displayed and referred to in the workplace.
- That they value building relationships with employees who are comfortable approaching them to discuss issues
- Employees who feel pride and ownership in their work and the work of the organisation

4. Always seeks meaningful data to guide decision-making

Leaders of Winning Organisations understand that good ideas and assumptions must be tested and validated. As resources are finite, it is only through the analysis of valid data that we can gain reliable estimates of outcomes. Without data, decision-making relies on experience and opinion. This makes the outcome less certain, as the loudest or most authoritative personality will usually drive decision-making and that will not necessarily result in the best outcome.

It's much easier to seek the data required to inform decision-making, than it is to execute a task. The commitment to finding data to support your decision-making greatly reduces the risk of unexpected outcomes. Valid data truly measures the characteristics that will provide value to achieve the required performance.

The SIPOC Model provides the framework to establish the measures needed to manage the performance of a process.

Leaders who understand the need to eliminate variation need to see process data represented graphically. Statistical control limits may be applied so you can better understand variability in the process.

Leaders will understand that no one criteria can adequately describe a process. A suite of measures must be considered to understand the performance of any process. These measures inform on not only what the outputs were, but how they were achieved and what the likely performance will be from the processes in the future.

The Goldilocks Factor—Balancing Risk and Reward in Decision-making

The Goldilocks Factor in leadership involves achieving the right balance between analysis, validation and speed of execution of the critical few high-leverage tasks.

The effective leaders of a winning organisation will ensure that a project isn't moved into execution phase too quickly. A clear understanding of value and what level of risk is acceptable supports timely decisions making.

If the fear of making a mistake dominates thinking, then it's likely that decision-making will become highly consensual and slow. Making mistakes must be considered a learning opportunity. Any potential harm from a mistake should be weighed against the potential value at risk. Controlling risk within acceptable limits that have been defined will limit the consequences of a mistake. Timeliness of decision making is important, if you wait too long, it's likely a more bullish competitor will get there ahead of you.

However, if you push projects that are flawed or not sufficiently defined into execution, it will result in cost overruns, delays in execution, rework and poorer returns on investment.

Winning organisations accept that mistakes will be made and that they must learn from them. Risk must be estimated in all decision-making. The coupling of risk and reward in a transparent way makes us realise that nothing is certain and allows for sensible discussion around the balance between the two. The open consideration of risk leads to ideas and strategies to control it within acceptable limits.

It's critical that the leadership creates a culture of open communication. This allows for fast decision-making where risks are identified, quantified and transparently considered as part of the risk and reward considerations.

The leadership must understand the risk and reward when analysing options and must be able to exercise sound judgement and act in a timely fashion without breaching any boundary conditions that have been set.

Leader or Entrepreneur?

All leaders are required to make decisions. The timeliness of this decision-making is important.

Good leaders must be able to make decisions at a point where there is still some risk and uncertainty about the likely outcome. Leaders must be able to judge the suitable level of risk. Take too long (*analysis paralysis*) and the organisation will stall. Make decisions too quickly and the level of mistakes will be high and confidence will wane.

An entrepreneur is said to be a person who organises and manages business with considerable initiative and risk. Classic stories of entrepreneurs typically involve seeing an opportunity, perhaps not seen by others, followed by an obsessive drive to make that opportunity become a reality. Often entrepreneurs suffer significant turmoil in their lives as they risk everything for the opportunity.

The life of the entrepreneur often has high peaks that crash to deep lows. Most organisations desire a more entrepreneurial spirit from their leaders. However, winning organisations must have the controls to understand and appropriately manage risk. In fact, entrepreneurs who manage to avoid the deep lows that come from taking high risks are often those fortunate enough to have had capable partner(s) with a non-entrepreneurial spirit.

Winning organisations must be able to generate value faster than their competitors. That requires leadership that can make decisions on balance with the right level of risk. They understand the personal characteristics of their leaders and add people to the team with other characteristics that add strength or provide controls to ensure any weaknesses are managed.

Winning organisations understand the strengths and weaknesses of their people and seek to build a balanced team where gaps or weaknesses are minimised. Someone who has a high-risk appetite will likely still have a high-risk appetite after years of coaching/counselling.

A chief financial officer I know recounted his experience of working with a highly entrepreneurial fellow who pulled off a deal that made him suddenly very wealthy. Despite the CFO having greater technical skills than the entrepreneur, he personally would never have been able to do the deal. The entrepreneur had risked everything, and more than he had, to secure the deal. If it had taken only days longer for the deal to materialise, not only would he have been ruined, his whole family would have been financially ruined, probably for the rest of their lives. The CFO recognised this extreme risk and would personally never have accepted it.

Winning organisations build teams that balance the individual characteristics of people to ensure risk is managed to an acceptable level.

Taking high risks or adopting accelerated decision-making with limited data may be appropriate provided that the level of commitment does not exceed your capacity to continue to thrive should things not go the way you planned.

Winning organisations with effective leadership in this characteristic will have:

- The discipline to ask for data that supports decisions
- Validation of the data and assumptions processes
- Analytical discipline to provide confidence estimates using best, worst and most likely estimates for critical variables
- A suite of measures that must be considered to fully understand a process
- Data analysis that is evident in the documentation of the decision-making process

5. Prioritises time to removing the barriers affecting your employees' ability to work to their full capability

Leaders in winning organisations understand their role in creating the right conditions so their employees can work to their full capability. The goal is to realise the value from people who willingly contribute their best every day. This can only be achieved when the leadership understands that this is part of their job.

Constant testing, review and action is required to learn and act as circumstances change. Leaders who understand the importance of their role in this aspect are invariably more open to listening, learning and building deeper, more productive working relationships with their employees. Conversely, leaders who do not understand this will be unable to access the full capability of their employees.

You need people with the right skills doing the right jobs at the right time and in the right way to the best of their ability every day. People who value and clearly understand their work make decisions in a timely manner to achieve the best outcomes for the organisation. Positive values-driven leadership is focused on delegating control to competent people. Teamwork is valued and should be a cultural feature of the organisation.

Effective leadership in an engaged workplace requires that:

- Leaders at all levels understand their roles
- Leaders at all levels have established standard work routines
- Leaders utilise planning methods from where the critical few goals/ tasks are derived
- Leaders utilise data/measures to track progress
- Leaders understand the values and demonstrate these consistently in the workplace

The role of a leader is to improve the performance of the team. A large portion of this should be focussed on influencing people, providing the right level of organisation and resources, and tracking progress with the team.

When a leader's behaviour is consistently perceived positively they will gain greater access to the true capability of their people. Engaged employees feel safe enough to contribute, empowered to act, are trusted to make decisions for the greater good of the team, feel proud about their work and openly share their ideas to find the best solutions to important problems.

This can only occur through effective communication and a belief that 'we are in it together' and 'we want to succeed'. People are motivated by sharing and providing an understanding of the vision and an invitation to be part of something important.

Example:

The new VP in an organisation had completed a strategy review and was in the process of holding briefing sessions with individual departments and shift teams. The VP had noted that it was difficult to get much feedback from 10–20 people involved in the sessions.

He was approached by an employee in the local supermarket. This employee enthusiastically thanked the VP for sharing the strategy during the briefing session. He went on to say that he now understood that the senior managers 'didn't know what was really going on'. Not what the VP was hoping he would say.

He explained that he had assumed that management knew about all the problems he experienced each day and that they didn't care enough to do anything about it. He was excited, because he now felt that management did care, and they simply had gaps in knowledge. He enthusiastically offered his help.

Put yourself in the shoes of a relatively new starter working in any organisation. It is reasonable for newer people to believe that longer serving people (particularly managers) must know much more than they do about the workplace. Therefore, it is reasonable for a new starter to assume that the manager must know about the problems that are obvious to them. When there is no action to correct chronic or obvious problems, it is understandable for the people to conclude that the manager must not care.

Example:

The president of an industrial business decided he would make a point to visit the workplace lunch rooms and washrooms, as he believed that what he found would reflect how people felt about the organisation.

What he found shocked him. There were years of neglect and squalor. He wondered how this could have happened. He realised that much more was required than just fixing the facilities before productive relationships with employees would flourish.

The poor facilities and their poor maintenance was a graphic reflection of the lack of care of the leaders over a prolonged time. The reality was that managers had not even entered the facilities for years and they even felt uncomfortable entering.

Barriers to employees working to their full capability can take many forms, such as:

- Poor systems that restrict initiative
- Lack of resources
- Lack of skills
- Lack of clear task and boundary limits
- Lack of information or information that isn't presented in the right way or at the right time
- The inappropriate use of power by others in the organisation for personal gain
- Processes that are out of control
- Quotas
- Lack of shared understanding of goals and priorities

In winning organisations, effective leaders who demonstrate this characteristic will have:

- Consistently demonstrated their commitment to helping people work to their full capability
- Structured feedback systems that are used to communicate and to share perspectives and ideas for improvement
- Employees who act confidently to address obstacles

6. Delegates authority to make control decisions to roles close to processes

If you want to offer a product or service with the least variability you need to act fast, when required, to minimise harmful variations. Winning organisations can't rely on lagging indicators at the process output stage. This is too late. The capability to control variation at the input and in-process stage is essential.

Leaders in winning organisations understand that to achieve the best results they need to create an environment where those employees closest to the process, those who will see change at the earliest stage, will have the right skills, knowledge, authority and accountability to take control action when required.

This requires a well-thought-out approach to process control, organisational design, communication and decision-making. The idea that decision-making be concentrated to senior management roles is incongruent with building a winning organisation. This characteristic consistently arises in organisations where lean thinking initiatives fail to realise their potential.

If you are a parent and you want your children to become successful adults, you need to provide the scope for the child to increase their discretion and responsibilities commensurate with their capability. Of course, good parents set limits based upon their assessment of the capability of the child, balancing long-term benefit and the risk of harm. Good parents maintain a caring involvement, so that they can intervene if these limits are challenged. If you don't parent this way, you'll probably create dependent or rebellious behaviour.

Winning organisations strive to fully utilise the capability of their people through adult to adult relationships. You can expect dysfunction in organisations where employees believe they're expected to park their brains at the gate. If people's brains are not engaged in productive work, they are most certainly still working on something.

Example:

A manager, when asked what his work was, said that, 'I am in charge, I run the place.'

What does that mean? What did this manager understand was the purpose of his role?

He believed he was there to make the decisions and his approach involved having people bring problems to him and he would decide on the appropriate

action. The operation of his business was chaotic, confused and there seemed to be no end of problems being brought to him.

He was focused on keeping things going rather than systematically improving his team's ability to achieve their goals. His relationship with his team reflected his distrust in their ability to make decisions and they didn't trust him either.

He was trying to do everyone else's decision-making, and while he was busy doing this, he was not doing the work that only the manager could do.

Example:

In the reconditioning department of a large industrial site there was constant conflict and poor performance. Changing managers did not seem to make any difference, until one manager talked to the whole team and carefully explained the aspirational performance required.

He told them that the organisation would consider outsourcing the work and he wanted the employees to submit a proposal outlining what the team thought it could achieve. They were given the scope to make whatever changes they required within legal, ethical and values limits.

Once they believed that change would occur and trusted that their proposal would be given fair consideration, they rolled up their sleeves and got involved. They submitted a proposal that included never-seen-before flexibility in rostering. The proposal submitted was close to the best of the proposals received from external sources.

The internal team was given the opportunity to prove what they could do. Within six months, they achieved best-in-world performance and this was with almost the same people.

Interestingly the proposal submitted listed only four people that would need re-assignment. These four hadn't caused trouble before, they were just poor performers and the team knew it better than the manager. But the previously troublesome employees had become the stand-out informal leaders. The leap from worst performing to world-class performing was achieved by setting a clear target, respectfully engaging the employees and allowing them appropriate discretion and control over their work.

In winning organisations, effective leaders demonstrating this characteristic will:

- Regularly spend time reviewing authorities and accountabilities to ensure that all employees have appropriate levels of authority to take ownership of their work
- Define escalation processes that ensure appropriate notification and timely action if a boundary limit is breached
- Make sure employees feel empowered to take the initiative to make decisions
- Ensure that budget authority and accountability is distributed, within limits, to every employee
- Engage in regular performance review discussions in each work area with each employee
- Ensure that employees taking measurements are authorised to make control changes within appropriate limits as they are accountable for the performance of their processes

7. Pursues the simplification and improvement of systems

Systems are designed to minimise variation through a series of steps that transform inputs into specified outputs. They are an extension of the leadership of the organisation and are like sub-conscious sub-routines of the organisational brain that organise how things get done.

In winning organisations, leaders recognise the important role of systems and the important work of leaders to simplify and improve them. Once we recognise that there are no perfect systems it will drive the pursuit of testing how well our systems are achieving their purpose and help us seek ways to improve them.

Unfortunately, employees in most organisations are subjected to poorly designed systems. These can be explicitly authorised or through lack of action, condoned by the leader. A poor system can continue to influence the performance of an organisation well after its original architect has gone.

A well-designed system has a clear purpose, is well-documented, including flowcharts. It has clearly defined role accountabilities and has established controls and measures to ensure that it's achieving its purpose. A well-designed system will provide a standardised way of doing something that reduces waste and duplication. Poorly-designed systems can retard initiative, impose non-value adding process steps, create confusion and waste resources.

Tools or software that supports certain transactions is often considered a system, even though they're not. For example, when asked about the safety reporting system at a site, the manager described a computer-based reporting system. This was a proprietary tool, and without a clear definition of roles, responsibilities and control measures, it did not make an effective system. The computer based tool was only part of the overall safety system.

It's the work of leadership to engage in the active review of systems and prioritise where to focus their improvement. Often organisations delegate the work of systems improvement too low in the organisation. System design needs to be led by senior management, as it is only at that level that the full context of the system can be assured. When senior management has only a cursory understanding on how such systems impact their organisation, they're missing a significant opportunity to positively influence how things operate.

Example:

Executives in a large industrial company were reviewing the annual budget and expressed concern over why IT costs were so high. One of the major costs was associated with the enterprise system— SAP. The IT executive was accountable for maintaining the system and budget. However, the IT department was not a major user of SAP. Someone asked why they needed it. The response was that the finance department wanted it.

'Don't we use it for maintenance and work management?' asked another. 'Since we put the system in how has our performance changed?'

All these good questions had vague answers.

'Who owns the system?' asked someone else.

'Well, we only support it,' said IT.

No one would accept that they owned the system, no one could answer what the value was from implementing it and no one knew whether spending more, or less, on it was a good idea.

Eventually, this sparked a review of what the system was being used for. This revealed a plethora of inconsistencies, including the use of multiple systems for the same purpose.

In the airline industry, a key value driver is a high utilisation of aircraft. Customers only value and pay for being transported from one location to another. The more paying customers in the air and the more hours the aeroplane is in the air, the greater the return on investment.

Reducing the turn-around time from landing to taking off is a key focus for improvement that has led to changes to boarding practices, carry-on luggage limits, in-flight cabin clean-up and check-in systems.

The purpose of a system is to transform or deliver a set of input components into output components in a repeatable way. Systems are an essential tool in the manager's kit to reduce or eliminate variation.

A winning organisation ensures that all core systems are clearly defined and flowcharted, including role authorities and accountabilities. The work of improving systems is recognised as important work in the roles of senior leaders. If you change the people and put them in the same system, the results will stay the same.

Example:

> *A technical expert raised concern that operators were not breaking up recycled lumps of raw materials into small enough pieces before returning the material to the process.*
>
> *During an industrial stoppage, he was required to work in the operator role. Towards the end of his first shift he returned some of the largest lumps ever seen into the process.*
>
> *He was asked why he was doing this, given his recent comments about the negative process impact from his actions. He replied that there was simply too much work to do to spend the time and energy breaking up the lumps.*

In this example, the system was incapable, and having done the work, the expert understood that the operators were simply getting the job done as best as they could within the current constraints. People will conform to system constraints quite rapidly.

A bad system works 24 hours a day. At least a bad manager goes home after eight to 12 hours.

When a system doesn't meet their needs, people identify it very quickly. So why are there so many poor systems? Common failings in system design stem from multiple or unclear definitions of purpose and the system not being formally documented.

Don't blame it on me, it is the system. This is a common response from people feeling constrained by a system that is not working effectively. It can also be symptomatic of a lack of clarity regarding who is the owner of a system and who is accountable for its performance. All systems are an extension of the organisation and by default, are owned by the senior leader, unless accountability has been clearly delegated to someone else.

An integral component of Lean Manufacturing is system improvement through value stream mapping. Value stream mapping focuses on identifying the value adding and non-value adding steps in processes. It then seeks the input of people involved with each to eliminate the non-value adding steps. This results in less waste, faster turnaround times, simplification and focused improvement on the process steps offering the greatest gain.

The 'way things are done' in an organisation can often evolve in an organic way. When this occurs, it is a "custom and practice" rather than a systematic.

In a winning organisation, the employees develop a culture for improvement that seeks to move productive customs and practices into productive systems. There is a regular review of authorised systems to find ways to make them simpler and able to achieve their purpose more effectively.

Unproductive, authorised systems are damaging to the culture of any organisation. When a system does not achieve its purpose well, makes the people who use it feel disrespected, or overly restricts their ability to use discretion, it can be worse than an unproductive leader.

Example:

A timekeeping system being used in a large organisation required each employee to complete a paper-based record of where each hour of each day was spent.

The records were then individually signed off by the area leader, then an administrator, then the head of the department before being filed. The total time to administer the system amounted to hundreds of man-hours per week. The administrator's entire role was about ensuring that every person submitted the form.

The leaders thought that the administrator was checking the accuracy of the forms; a kind of audit and compliance role. The department head thought that leaders used the system to manage their people and in-work planning.

Upon review, it was revealed that no one ever used the information. All it resulted in was a large room full of bundles of records that were thought to be used by the HR department.

The cost of this system was estimated at close to $500k per annum. No one owned it and hence, no one was accountable for whether it was adding value or not. It was decided to replace this system with an absence reporting system that was initiated by the team leader for employees who were absent. Eventually this was further automated using personalised access cards, such that any anomalies were reported to the person accountable for action if required, which almost completely relieved the management burden. A cultural consequence of this change was increased trust and more flexible working arrangements that benefitted employees and the organisation.

Every organisation will have customs and practices, and many will have systems that are there to improve the consistency of how routine processes are operated to create value.

Some of the key systems that would be expected in any sizable organisation include:

- Financial profit and loss (P&L)
  o Cost management
  o Material supply
  o Approvals to commit funds
- Market development
- Risk management
  o Enterprise/projects/task level
  o Health, safety and environment
  o Change management
  o Insurances and licence to operate (legal)
- Quality
  o Specifications
  o Dealing with non-conformance and customer feedback
- People
  o Workplace terms and conditions
  o Hiring/firing
  o Talent development
- Induction
- The way we work
  o Skills and training
  o Performance management
  o Engagement 'gap to perfect'
  o Communications
  o Knowledge management
  o Impacts of variation
- Effective planning
  o Standard work procedures
  o it-for-purpose engineering
  o Reliability-centred maintenance
  o Work execution
- Analyse and improve
  o Input/in-process/output measures
  o Leading measures focused on the work
  o Customer feedback
  o Root cause analysis

Macdonald Systems Leadership provides a useful guide for systems design and improvement. Macdonald identified 20 systems design questions that provide improved clarity of purpose, how the system creates value, role responsibilities, how the system reflects positive values, how much it will cost and what measures and controls will be incorporated to ensure that its performance can be measured.

If you want to design effective systems, you need a clear business case with measures and controls built in to assess its performance. The value created by any system needs to justify the cost.

Clarity of purpose in the design of a system curbs the inclination to add non-value adding functionality. Effective controls designed into a system allow its owner to determine whether it's being used as it was intended. When system controls are weak, the owner cannot determine whether poor system performance is due to the wrong theory in its design or that it's simply not being followed.

Example:

A large government performance and development system, measured the number of completed annual reviews to assess how well it was being used. The logging of a review was completed by department leaders.

The data suggested that less than 50% of reviews were completed each year. Many employees stated that they had never completed a performance review. Leaders and employees consistently said that the system was just a waste of time. It was impossible to determine whether the lack of compliance in following the system or the system design itself was the problem.

A control measure had been developed giving the leader the ability to state that a review had taken place without any verification from the team member required. This contributed to the misinformation, as leaders simply clicked the box saying that they considered a review had taken place. Given that, in most cases, the system was not even producing output, it was possible that it was not required at all and was just wasting scarce resources.

Lean thinking is often thought of as being applicable to manufacturing, where speeding up production lines is a key value driver. In lean process mapping exercises, each step is assessed to determine whether it is adding value or not. Eliminating non-value steps in process design drives faster, better, cheaper production.

Just as all processes have variation, all processes contain non-value adding steps. Non-value adding steps may be caused by many factors, including not having identified a cost-effective solution. It helps focus improvement efforts if you clearly understand whether a process step adds value or not.

Winning organisations understand the importance of effective systems and actively engage with the people who are impacted by any system in order to improve its design and productivity. It is standard work for senior leaders in winning organisations to improve its systems.

In winning organisations, effective leaders demonstrating this characteristic will have:

- Senior leadership who invest in creating and improving systems
- A clear purpose and value proposition for all authorised systems
- A flowchart of all authorised systems
- Defined roles and responsibilities within the system
- A system design that considers how people interacting with it will feel (linked to core values)
- Clear owner and effective measures and controls to assess how well it achieves its purpose
- A clear understanding of the value/cost proposition of systems
- The involvement of stakeholders in the review and improvement of systems
- An understanding of SIPOC Model
- Evidence of where systems provide a competitive edge for the organisation

8. Actively encourages open, transparent and face-to-face communication

Leaders recognise their role in promoting open communications and in ensuring that a preference for face-to-face communication is met. Only the leadership can create the environment for differences in viewpoints or understanding to be shared, challenged, clarified and resolved effectively and efficiently.

Open communications provide a licence to respectfully disagree with a viewpoint expressed by more senior people in an organisation. If you have the confidence and trust to express yourself, it is more likely to create a culture which produces better solutions and a more aligned understanding of decisions.

It's the work of leaders to create the safe environment to share and explore different ideas. Leaders need to have the self-confidence and courage to invite others to challenge or disagree with their point of view.

Communication is fraught with opportunities for error. Face-to-face communication is the most effective, as with eye contact, you'll communicate more effectively. Body language, tone, emotions and empathic feedback, such as nodding the head, greatly enrich the conversation.

Open, transparent, face-to-face communication is likely to lead to greater alignment and commitment to act when a decision is made, or tasks are assigned.

In winning organisations, effective leaders demonstrating this characteristic will have:

- Regular face-to-face meetings to discuss progress on goals and objectives
- Employees who feel comfortable asking questions and making suggestions to leaders
- Information that is shared as leaders seek to create a share and learn culture
- Employees who will approach senior leaders in the workplace to discuss work

9. Positively demonstrates the six core values through their behaviour

Effective leaders in winning organisations behave in a positive manner in relation to core values. *Macdonald's System Leadership* describes core values as care for the well-being of others, respect, trust, fairness, courage and honesty.

Leadership behaviours will, over time, have a significant effect on the culture of the organisation. Winning organisations require teamwork and the engagement of its employees which, in turn, must be based upon behaviour that is positively perceived against the core values.

In any organisation, the most important work of the leader (or manager) concerns people. If you are a manager that assigns work to employees, then you are in a leadership role.

It's equally important to keep in mind that without a customer there is no business, and customers are people.

People don't react like machines. You can't simply turn them on and off. People make choices and they choose how much effort and conscious thought to devote to any subject.

To access the conscious thought of people, leaders need to be interesting and relevant to them. If you want to access your employees' true capability, you need to progress from being merely interesting to a relationship where thoughts, collaborative will, and the potential to disagree or propose alternative ideas are fundamental. The first step in engagement is to recognise and respect the person as an individual. In winning organisations, all people ensure that everyone is treated with respect.

Example:

The president of a medium-sized international company called a meeting to discuss the compliance of his team with the annual performance review process.

He started by saying that he 'wanted compliance with this HR stuff'. It was clear that he neither owned nor held much interest in what was intended to be an important performance system. The response represented how the organisation viewed its people.

In this example, senior managers in the organisation held a view that 'people work' was predominantly a skill-based function of HR.

The CEO of another large international organisation was personally involved in developing core systems. He was particularly interested in how the grievance system reflected the organisations values.

He was adamant on one feature of the system design—that any employee could ultimately escalate their grievance to the CEO if they felt that it had not been resolved to their satisfaction by other means.

Some people were incredulous that the CEO would make such a commitment. The system gained credibility when an employee in an entry level role asked for his situation to be reviewed by the CEO. The employee, who was clinging to his job after a string of misdemeanours, was provided with flights and accommodation to have his grievance heard at the head office.

What did this say about the respect for all employees' rights to a fair go? The behaviour of the CEO through his actions and through the system design itself, clearly demonstrated respect, fairness and care, not just for the person using the system, but to all employees interested in what was happening. Trust is proportional to the behaviours of leaders and how they prioritise their time to engage their people.

It is not difficult to predict which of the two organisations referenced above was able to tap into the true capability of its people.

A winning organisation can only be achieved by accessing and organising the collective will and capabilities of its people. If the senior management don't understand this, or don't behave in a manner that reinforces this, then you will not become a winning organisation.

The behaviours of the senior leadership will have the greatest influence on the culture within the organisation. Leaders of winning organisations value and behave supportively regarding:

- Listening, observing and sharing
- Clarifying
- Demonstrating care of the well-being of people
- Always respecting others
- Asking for people to provide feedback on how to improve personally and as an organisation.
- Authorising employees to have a voice and role in eliminating waste

It's important to assess what your leaders devote their time to, as people observe and assess what they do against core values that underpin all sustainable communities. A leader who says she/he cares about people and safety and then spends all their time focusing on costs and production will be viewed negatively against core values.

Example:

A large multi-national organisation identified that, to become the number one company in the world, it needed to embrace operational excellence.

To gain an impression of the current feelings towards the company, employees were asked to draw a picture that represented their working life.

A picture can tell a thousand words. One drawing said so much—it showed a giant person with a large mouth and no ears yelling down to many ant-sized figures with disproportionately large ears and small mouths. The ant-sized figures represented the employees. Clearly, whoever drew the picture did not feel engaged by their leaders. Another drawing depicted employees as being part man, part dog and part slave!

Values such as caring for others, respect and trust cannot be faked and must be demonstrated regularly. It is not what managers say but what they do that matters. The choices they make in difficult situations or in a crisis are particularly telling.

Beware of false prophets when seeking to create a new culture. It is common for people to learn the buzz words or sprout verbatim quotations because they have worked out what the boss wants to hear.

In every organisation there is always significant inertia from people who have acquired power within the prevailing culture. Changing the behaviours of the people who hold power requires considerable effort and persistence from the leader.

The CEO that reviewed the grievance understood how important it was that he followed through on his commitment. He understood that the whole organisation was watching to see if his actions matched his words. He cared about people and could see the potential to gain from a values-driven approach to leadership.

A key characteristic of a winning organisation is a genuine commitment from its leadership to prioritise and commit time to create the right organisational culture and behavioural norms.

Values

Values are defined as attributes that have worth to a person or group of people.

There is a saying— 'People will forget what you did, people will forget what you said, however, people will remember how you made them feel.' Creating an inspired team of people working to a common goal requires that they feel positive and proud of their association with that team.

How leaders behave sets the cultural tone for an organisation. Terms like emotional intelligence and humility are attributed to great leaders. These attributes reflect an understanding that how the work is done is at least as important as the immediate results.

People ask questions regarding what they see and how they are impacted. People want to know why certain things are done in certain ways. They want to understand the motive behind the behaviour. Then they choose where and how they allocate their discretionary effort.

The human brain is continually making interpretations and judgements based upon beliefs about the world. Beliefs are formed from experience and new learning. People ascribe worth to what they observe through their lens or beliefs, and they will assess the worth or merit of what they observe against these core values. Employees make value judgements every day based on what they see and experience, and how it made them feel.

The ability of a leader to influence their team will be different if they are perceived to be honest rather than dishonest.

Macdonald in the *Systems Leadership* text identifies six core values upon which all productive societies are built. They are:

- Trust
- Honesty
- Fairness
- Courage
- Care for the well-being of others
- Respect for the dignity of others

People observe and interpret the worth of a person's behaviour against these core values through their set of beliefs. When people perceive a behaviour or event positively with reference to their core values, they are likely to give it positive recognition.

Leaders who are consistently perceived to behave positively regarding the core values are likely to benefit from a more engaged commitment from their team.

Values cannot be taken for granted; just because someone says so doesn't make it so. The evidence is in how people respond to situations.

These values are often referred to when people describe their leaders. People are constantly being observed and measured by others against these core values as they ascribe positive or negative judgements based upon their beliefs and context.

People have good 'bullshit detectors' and so people attempting to communicate or behave in a fake or contrived manner are usually found out quickly.

People are likely to accept difficult decisions when the decision rates positively against their values, even if they personally suffer hardship from the decision. They will not accept a decision if they view it negatively against one or more core value.

People can accept decisions on the overall balance of assessment against the values. The 'on balance' capability extends to overall assessments; in the event of a slip-up or mistake, a person with a good track record will usually receive more leeway than a person with a bad track record.

The Values Continua Model can be used to assess how people who observe a certain behaviour through a certain set of beliefs will ascribe positive or negative judgement on its worth.

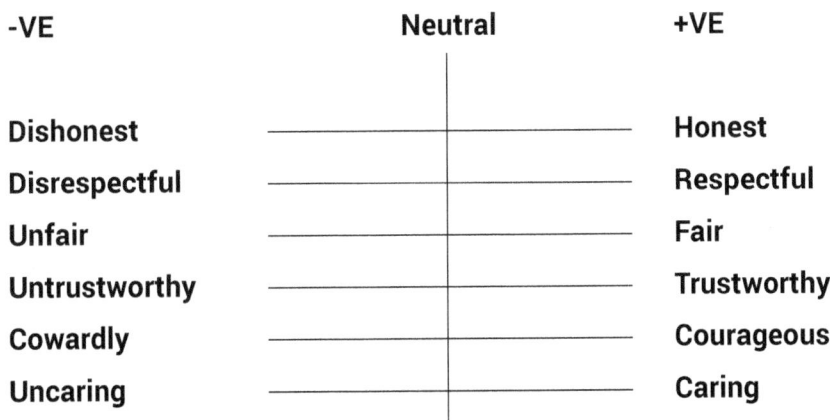

-VE	Neutral	+VE
Dishonest		Honest
Disrespectful		Respectful
Unfair		Fair
Untrustworthy		Trustworthy
Cowardly		Courageous
Uncaring		Caring

Figure 5: Values Continua Model for use in assessing perceptions of behaviours

If a group of people believe that all politicians are liars encounter a politician who avoids providing a direct answer to a question, they will conclude that he/she has something to hide. The hesitancy to provide a direct answer would likely be interpreted as evidence of untrustworthiness, dishonesty and cowardice.

A group of people who believe that politicians are ordinary members of society might observe the same behaviour and assess the politician as being honest (not knowing the answer), courageous (not just giving any answer because it is easier), trustworthy (not presuming to have all the answers).

Another observer who believes that the journalist who asked the question of the politician to be devious and seeking to entrap the politician, may be neutral in their assessment of the politician and judge the journalist as being untrustworthy and unfair.

It's important to describe how the core values will be demonstrated in your organisation. You must describe clearly how the values will be evidenced in the behaviours of the leadership.

As always in winning organisations, the clearer the understanding of how the values are demonstrated, the greater the potential for alignment, consistency and effective communication. Alignment and consistency around values allows people to anticipate and relate to each other more effectively. Positive organisations will have people who are proud to be part of it and who are motivated to drive out behaviours that are inconsistent or reflect negatively against the core values.

Ideas and methods can be copied or replicated more easily than a positive value-driven culture. A well-established culture based upon core values that supports an organisation's vision will contribute to sustaining efficiencies and flexibilities in how the team is able to communicate and respond to changing needs.

An example of how powerful a clear set of values can be to an organisation is in safety. It is a natural desire of most organisations to ensure that no one who works for them is harmed. In organisations where the leadership truly devotes their time and priority to act in support of a zero-harm philosophy to work, the safety results are overwhelmingly better than peer organisations without this stated, and most importantly, practised value.

Leaders who can demonstrate behaviours that are perceived positively against the core values will be able to access the so-called 'hearts and minds' of people more effectively. A winning organisation is only attainable through the collective and aligned efforts of its people over time.

Sustaining high levels of safety is only possible when the 'care for the well-being of others' value is accepted and practised by the workforce. Values are only real when evidenced in how people act and in the choices that they make. The true test of the extent to which a value is held is when it is challenged. In these circumstances, it will be apparent what is really important to the person.

Stephen Covey described the notion of an emotional bank account in his book, *Six Habits of Highly Effective People*. Covey relates that people can look at the weight of evidence over time, rather than just one data point, when it comes to how they rate that person's worth. For example, a person who has demonstrated a track record of being honest is likely to have established the perception of being an honest person. The person's track record would be considered if a single questionable behaviour was observed. Of course, if there is a subsequent trend in behaviours that are perceived as dishonest, eventually the person will no longer be considered honest. People are constantly observing and building perceptions that relate to the worth of the people with whom they interact.

Example:

In a workplace that was not doing too well, the leadership was contemplating a reduction in staff. Each leader was asked to rank employees from best to worst based upon set criteria of performance and potential value to the organisation.

The first response of the leaders was that ranking people was inappropriate; that every person was an individual that could not be summed up as a number.

When pushed to try and complete the ranking, every leader was able rank people from excellent to poor in their team with clear reasoning in less than half an hour. This example demonstrates that the leaders had been gathering data on the relative worth of their people on an ongoing basis through their normal interactions and observations.

A perfectly aligned assessment on the worth of a person or organisation is unlikely. Most people will accept the imperfection of humanity and be guided by the overwhelming evidence of behaviours they have observed over time when assessing the worth of the person or organisation.

It is important to recognise that not all people observing the same thing are likely to interpret it the same way. People will interpret the worth of what they see through the beliefs they have and within the context of their situation or environment.

Values will be tested in any organisation and actions taken or not taken will establish what is really valued. If a leader was to encourage the undermining of a safety standard to meet a customer delivery, the belief in a zero-harm value is likely to be doubted along with the leader's credibility.

When a leader in the organisation behaves in a manner contrary to its values, everyone will see what happens. There will be consequences for both positive and negative perceptions of behaviour. The consequences of negative perceptions can't always be seen, as negative perceptions are likely to diminish commitment. Diminished commitment can result in people choosing to do just enough rather than the best they can.

In the case of President Richard Nixon and the Watergate scandal, it was more his dishonesty once the scandal broke, rather than the scandal itself, that galvanised people in the enduring negative perception of his character.

The power of thinking from another person's perspective

People don't like change when it is forced upon them by others, particularly if they perceive that their interests will be disadvantaged by the change.

People want to feel valued and successful. When they feel that a change is valuable, that they can contribute to it and benefit from it, they generally become enthusiastically involved.

Taking the time to consider the perspective of another person who is likely to be affected by change provides powerful insight about that person's perspective.

When leaders take the time to consider the perspective of people impacted by a change they are likely to adjust their approach so that change will gain greater acceptance.

Example:

Managers in a resource company decided that greater emphasis on risk assessment by employees working in the frontline roles was needed to eliminate harmful incidents.

The managers believed it was essential that each employee carried and used a booklet to assess and decide how to control hazards. The process, if followed, would likely eliminate or greatly reduce incidents involving harmful uncontrolled energy releases.

When the managers considered the perspective of the frontline workers in implementing the change, they realised that it would be disrespectful to

introduce it without some workshops that shared key information, present the reason why the change was required and why it would work.

They also identified a possible concern that frontline employees might view the booklet as something management could use to discipline those who made a mistake or did not write things down. When they considered these perspectives, the management ran workshops and asked the employees to provide input into how to ensure that the books would be used effectively.

In following this approach, it took longer to roll-out the change. However, its understanding and acceptance was high. An agreement was reached that the booklets would be audited by managers from time to time and any deficiencies would, in the first instance, be referred to a mixed role committee that would then advise on an action they considered would confidently prevent a recurrence.

The high degree of acceptance of the change was due entirely to the process used and respectful inclusion of contributions from those most affected. The purpose was clear, the motive noble and the system contributed to fewer people being injured.

The simple step of putting yourself in the other person's shoes will lead to ideas on how to lead the people more effectively and will widen the breadth of options available for the team.

It is said that you cannot change a person's beliefs, rather, you must create a new belief. Imagine all your beliefs as pages in a file that cannot be removed. You can only add new pages to the top of the file. If a person holds a belief that 'all people with power cannot be trusted' and you are a person with power who is seeking to gain that person's trust, you would need to create a new belief, something like, 'All people with power cannot be trusted, except this person, who seems trustworthy'.

By considering how the person might interpret a certain action you are able to modify your approach to avoid creating a reaction that was unintended.

People will often use symbols, slogans and sayings that reflect the culture of an organisation. Culture is defined as a group of people who share a common belief.

Example:

> *An organisation was at risk of going out of business due to obsolete technology and a high degree of conflict within the workforce. It decided to attempt to map the cultures that existed. The idea was to reinforce the existing positive beliefs and create new ones to replace the existing negative beliefs that were holding back the organisation.*
>
> *Some of the negative beliefs that were identified included 'them and us' (referring to staff and wages paid employees) and 'good pay for shit work' (meaning that the employees felt they were paid more than fairly to do work that was unpleasant and unenjoyable).*
>
> *By looking at how things were done through the lens of these beliefs it was possible to see many symbols, systems and behaviours that were reinforcing negative beliefs that could be addressed. The need to make significant and lasting improvement could only be achieved by redirecting the negative energy into positive aligned teamwork.*
>
> *By systematically demonstrating that all employees would be treated positively regarding the core values, the leadership created a new belief of 'one team of people working together for the benefit of all stakeholders'. This provided a stark contrast with the old belief of 'them and us'.*
>
> *Having experienced the consequences of the negative belief, employees were even more motivated to do what they could to support the new 'one team' approach. Today, this organisation has continued to defy the economy of scale pressures mainly due to the culture that began over 23 years ago and has been valued and nurtured ever since.*

An investment is required to help new and existing employees create an understanding of how core values should be exhibited within an organisation. Without discussion, exploration and 'learning together', it is likely that the values will not become a real feature in how the organisation behaves.

Relationships build when employees hear first-hand from the leaders in your organisation about the vision, how it all works and feel a personal connection with them. A relationship built upon mutual respect between the individual and the leadership is fundamental to creating a sense of belonging and shared commitment to the team.

The development of shared understanding and language supports improved communication, clarity and efficiency. When a person understands the purpose and context of the vision, not to mention their behavioural expectations, how

their role fits and how decisions are made, they are more likely to be engaged as they will realise they have a voice and an open relationship with the leaders.

Example:

The managers of a global business were invited to a workshop session. The opening address was conducted by the vice president and he opened with an explanation that the organisation had decided that teamwork was an essential element in all roles.

The VP then told the forum that if they weren't team players they should consider finding a new job as there would be no tolerance of non-team players. This caused every person to question what kind of team player they were.

The session went on to outline examples and scenarios that constituted good teamwork and those that did not. This approach was effective in making it clear that teamwork was a requirement for how people were expected to work and created a common understanding amongst the leadership as to what it meant.

Example:

A manufacturing organisation had the opportunity to increase productivity by engaging its employees' more effectively.

After a period of consultation, workshops and research, the executive team decided on a set of values that would become common across the organisation. Posters, videos and billboards were installed that displayed the values at prominent locations around sites.

After several years, surveys identified that employees did not think that the values had been incorporated in day-to-day interactions. Further investigations revealed that most people could not clearly describe what they were supposed to do with the values.

An induction at a new site included discussion and examples on how the values could be positively or negatively represented. They were reinforced in participative exercises carried out by the employees. At the end of the induction all participants passed a competency assessment that confirmed they understood the values and knew how to apply them for the benefit of themselves and the organisation.

The values were further reinforced back in the workplace through performance reviews, toolbox meetings and values recognition awards.

Gradually, the workforce learnt to embody and protect the positive behaviours of the values in a way that provided competitive advantage.

Changing Behaviours

People often ask how to change the behaviour of the 30% of people in the organisation who seem to resist change.

The easiest group of people to convince of the need of change are the ones who already believe the change is required (usually at least 30% of the population). Then there is the population that holds no strong conviction on an issue and can be influenced (usually also around 30%).

The difficult people from a leader's perspective are those with different beliefs. They may perceive that the change will disadvantage them or don't understand the need for change. If people have invested significant personal energy into a certain position on an issue, change can threaten their self-esteem and personal credibility.

You can gain important insights on how to make a change by understanding people's beliefs and knowing how the present situation came about. Any change has the greatest chance of being accepted if you find solutions that will be perceived positively against the core values.

It is said that people need several points of confirmation before committing to change. Macdonald describes the need to create dissonance (where previous models no longer seem to be providing reliable predictions of what's happening) before a person will begin to create new beliefs.

Malandro describes four states of mind (content, denial, confusion, reform) that a person must move through before adopting a new belief. If a person is content or in the denial stage, they will not make a change

To move from denial to confusion requires that the person recognise a change is affecting them and they are no longer able to predict what is going on as their previous beliefs don't seem to work anymore. The confused person is looking for a solution and at this point is receptive to ideas that may lead to a new belief or solution.

The person then moves to the reformation stage, which is where change can take place. Once predictability is restored the person can return to being content.

In business it is said that the average number of contacts required before securing a new customer is five. Most organisations give up after three. People need weight of evidence, time and feedback from other sources before accepting a new proposition.

The change is more likely to be accepted if the leader can genuinely answer the following questions:

- What is in it for me?
- What is in it for you?
- What is in it for us?
- What is in it for the wider organisation or community?

If the person does not value the change, then they will not exert effort to support it.

Highly effective leaders listen carefully to people. There is a huge difference between saying 'I will try' to do something and saying, 'I will do something'. The difference between try and will, could be due to a lack of clarity on how to do it or that the person is unsure of their commitment to the task. It could also be uncertainty as to how this commitment will fit with other commitments. It could also be uncertainty regarding what can be achieved from completing the task.

In the process of seeking commitment and clarity from a person, the leader will likely learn new information that may improve the plan and increase the probability of alignment and success.

Even when a commitment to change is achieved, there is still likely to be significant and sustained effort required to translate that commitment into action.

It usually takes at least six weeks for a person to form a new habit. Even once a habit or behaviour is established, some form of control action is essential to keep things within an acceptable level of variation. It is possible for people to delude themselves about progress without objective feedback. For example, it is decided that scales need to be calibrated every 24 hours. So, re-calibration is made an important task. For the first two weeks the re-calibration is done every 24 hours, however, in the third week a process upset meant that some re-calibrations were missed. If there is no control action that assesses adherence to the frequency chosen, then eventually the practices will relapse. The control action may be an audit that is conducted to review the re-calibration records and raise an alert if one is missed.

For example, if a person decided to make changes to diet and lifestyle to lose weight then it is essential that they weigh themselves periodically to assess their progress. Then they can review their plan, test assumptions and adjust.

Leaders must focus on what they can control. The leader can only control what they do. They cannot make another person change. They can convey the need for change and relate what they'll do if the change is not achieved. Being clear on the consequences if change is not made can be a powerful control action. Controls are even more robust when incorporated into an effective system.

In winning organisations, effective leaders demonstrating this characteristic will have:

- A clear set of organisational values that reflect the six core values
- Behaviour that demonstrates a positive view of the values
- Pride and participation in the organisation at all levels
- Flexibility and speed of action that is underpinned by a clear and shared understanding of how the organisation works to achieve its goals

10. Accepts responsibility for improving the performance of the team

The managers of winning organisations understand that they are the authorised leaders of their teams. They understand and accept that they are accountable to the organisation and the team they represent for improving performance.

It's not acceptable for them to simply maintain the status quo. They are continuously motivated to seek improvement in how they can meet organisational goals and objectives more effectively.

Does your organisation have the right people doing the right work in the right way at the right time? WOM requires a clear connection of roles to processes and how they create value that only leaders can provide. How does one role fit with others, systems and processes? This must be understood by the leader as he/she is accountable for the cost and value created by the work.

The leader is also accountable for overall team performance and particularly the ability to deliver improved outcomes. Better, faster and cheaper expectation must be a characteristic in a winning organisation. To meet this accountability fairly, the leader must have the authority to select, recognise and reward each team member based upon performance. The performance of the team always sets the context for the performance of the individuals who make up the team.

Example:

A well-established government organisation became exposed to an open tender for services that it had been providing for over 15 years. The tender process revealed that some providers in the market now had the capability to provide the service at half the cost and in half the time as the established provider. The work was awarded to the much more competitive proposal.

As a learning exercise, the organisation that lost the tender attempted to redesign processes to determine what changes needed to be made. One of the problem areas was productivity, as the manager had reasonably assumed that his current employee productivity should be applied to the tender.

The identification of this issue revealed that the organisation tolerated poor performers. The manager had been frustrated over many years as he had attempted to address poor performance to no avail and had given up trying. Not only had this resulted in an additional overhead, the frustration had infiltrated the whole team and people had accepted working to the lowest common denominator.

The lack of authority allocated to the manager had kept him from addressing poor performance. This contributed to the company's lack of competitiveness and lack of acceptance of accountability by the manager for the team's performance.

Many organisations invest in leadership training for their management without ever reaching a clear and common understanding of what is required of a leader. In winning organisations, the work of a leader is clearly defined and understood by all employees.

The use of leadership framework can greatly improve consistency and quality of leadership. A leader must be able to communicate the goals and objectives effectively, as well as develop plans, assign tasks, and review and improve performance.

Team Leadership Framework

To achieve a clear understanding of how roles and responsibilities fit together requires a common understanding of them. This must be reinforced with a consistent approach over time.

Providing a clear and simple outline of what everyone can expect from their leaders allows all employees to provide feedback on how well they feel their leaders are executing their roles. The following simple model has proven to be effective and helps de-mystify what is leadership.

LEADERSHIP FRAMEWORK

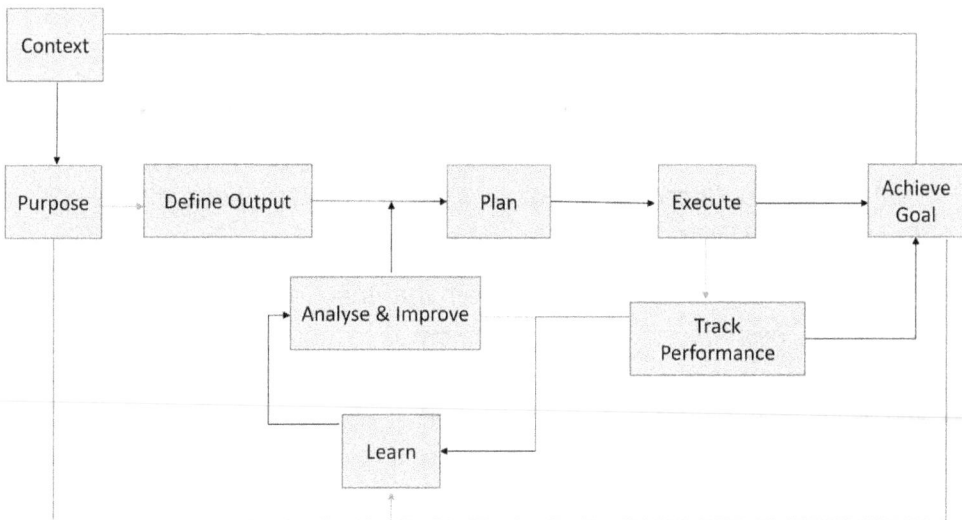

Figure 6: Team leadership framework

This team leadership framework sets the standard expectation for not only the leadership, but the whole organisation. It provides a common understanding of the leadership process and its work. It is also a practical framework for discussing required behaviours that positively reflect the values of the organisation.

Context

The context provides the team with the understanding of where their purpose fits in the bigger picture. This enables the team to exercise discretion should an opportunity arise to create value outside their specific purpose.

There will always be variation and unforeseen obstacles in achieving goals. In these situations, people will have opportunity to make decisions and innovate. Understanding context enables the team to make decisions more effectively.

Purpose

You can set the focus by providing a clear measurable purpose statement that defines the team's common objective.

It is better if the purpose statement doesn't contain the word 'and'. Usually when the word 'and' is used in a purpose statement, it suggests that there may be more than one purpose. It is better to assign multiple tasks or objectives than to mix up objectives in one purpose statement.

Example:

In a large industrial organisation, the HR department intended to design a best practice performance and development system to be used in rewarding performance and developing talent. However, performance and development are clearly different purposes.

In this instance, the result was a system that tried to meet two objectives and failed. The predictable bias of leaders was to focus on development, as this is always an easier area of discussion. Eventually, separate performance and development systems were developed.

Define Output

A clear set of measurable outputs that are time-bound should be defined from the purpose statement. This allows the planning process to develop pathways which can achieve the required outputs.

Plan

Planning involves gathering ideas or possible actions and the analysis of data to estimate the resulting output. A plan is the set of actions or steps that the leader has chosen as the best way to achieve the output.

It is the leaders work to decide the pathway. However, it is the work of the team to contribute ideas and solutions during planning.

Execution

In execution phase, the leader must assign the tasks and resources to the team as they'd planned. Each person is accountable for executing their tasks according to this plan.

Track Performance

Nothing is a certainty. There will always be variation in how tasks are completed and in the output achieved. Tracking progress during the execution of the work will let the team know whether they're on track to achieve their goals or whether an intervention is required.

Analyse and Improve

The analysis of data allows for predictions and theories to be developed. Ideas for improvement are defined and analysed to estimate value should an idea be converted into a task.

This step provides essential input into planning or when contemplating an intervention if the performance of the process moves outside the limits set.

Learn

This step involves the capture of knowledge that has been gained throughout the process. This knowledge can then be used to analyse and improve things. The Learn phase also seeks to lock in gains by creating a documented record that can be accessed by the team. This knowledge can be used to improve and to develop robust controls to prevent causes of harmful variations from reoccurring.

Achieve Goal

The goal or task is achieved once it has met all the performance requirements. The leader recognises the achievement of the team and individuals within the team and documents any further learnings for future improvement.

The adoption of the Team Leadership Model alone does not make a person a good leader. However, it does help leaders to be more consistent and effective.

Many leadership development programs focus on leadership style and motives. While this is often useful, it doesn't ensure a consistent approach. The team leadership framework proposed accommodates different styles and is simple to understand and apply. Having a clear understanding of what is required from leaders is critical to winning organisations.

Team Leadership Behaviours

Leader

- Explain the context & purpose
- Identify critical issues
- Encourage contributions
- Plan and assign tasks
- Review
- Coach

Team

- Understanding the context & purpose
- Ask - Share - Learn
- Contribute ideas and solutions to plan
- Clarify and accept tasks assigned
- Demand Review
- Accept coaching

Listen – Collaborate – Seek improvement

Figure 7: Team leadership behaviours

Example:

In a leadership training course, the leader of a team excitedly claimed success in getting his team through the series of challenges.

He had been on one side of the final barrier and the rest of the team was on the other. The leader did not consider himself to be a team member, so had moved forward with a plan that left him stranded.

All team leaders are team members and it is a mistake to think otherwise. Leaders or managers have no role in isolation from the team. They are often part of more than one team.

All leaders must listen and collaborate as they seek improvement in their own capability and performance and that of the team they are privileged to lead.

I have heard the argument that it is not necessary to appoint a leader in empowered teams. However, at some point, decisions need to be made. Some of these will be in the best interest of the team or organisation and cannot be reached by consensus in a reasonable timeframe. In these instances, a leader emerges that most team members are willing to follow.

Leaderless teams become teams with an informal leader or various leaders, depending on the circumstance. These informal leaders are likely to be poorly connected to the organisational goals and will lack the authority and capability to meet the full requirements of their role. In fact, informal leaders are likely to have to rely on unauthorised methods of reward and recognition.

This is not to say that situational leadership is not desirable. It's a very good way to develop capability and to utilise it within the team. Situational leadership works well when the authorised team leader delegates his/her authority to another with the appropriate communication and continued involvement of the authorised leader.

A good leader cannot be the technical expert on all matters that the team may encounter and does not have all the answers. He/she must harness the full capability of the team to achieve their goals as required, or better than required, where possible.

The team leadership behaviours template shown in figure 7 describes the behaviours required for a winning organisation. All employees are expected to demonstrate these behaviours. 'Listen', 'collaborate' and 'seek improvement' apply to all employees. Collaboration involves seeking out knowledge from

others, learning and applying knowledge gained, and sharing and contributing further knowledge that you acquired.

These behaviours improve communication and contribute to an increased collective rate of learning and improvement.

Decision-making

The leadership must make decisions in a timely manner that support the purpose of the organisation. Leadership in decision-making requires:

- The use of data
- Theories that can predict future cause and effect relationships
- An understanding of the important levers for the organisation
- Courage to commit to an opportunity when others want more analysis

The work of the leadership in decision-making requires the ability to draw out the contribution of others. The leader's role is to define the goal or objective of the team clearly and to gather sufficient knowledge from available sources, including the team itself.

Once a decision is made, the leader must ensure that all people affected by the decision understand the implications for their work priorities. Often there is more work involved in communicating the decision and ensuring alignment than in the decision itself.

Example:

A large resources company asked people in roles on the operating floor if they were aware of a recent decision by the managing director to reduce spending.

The response was, 'By the time we find out about any big boss decisions, the boss will already have been changed, so we just ignore what we hear from management.' This response reflected significant problems in the organisation around communication and consistency of purpose from senior management.

Leading Change

It is common to hear the phrase, 'Nobody likes change'. People do, however, face change constantly throughout their life. People have inquisitive minds and they are always looking for ways to become more successful.

When change is imposed by others this can create fear and resistance in people as they experience a lack of control over the future and worry about what the change may foreshadow. When change feels like the imposition of someone's will or challenges your vision of your future, it is predictable that you will object to it.

Example:

In a refining business, a high number of people were employed to handle heavy metal anodes, with a consequent high injury rate and high cost.

When the management considered bringing in automations to carry out the work, they involved the workforce and the union officials who represented them. The first response from the union officials was that they could not support the change as it would lead to a loss of jobs for workers. However, when management provided a clear picture of the importance of the project in addressing injuries and reducing costs that would allow for employment growth in other areas, the union officials became more aligned with the direction.

Once this alignment had been achieved, rather than resist change, the workforce went that extra yard to ensure that the changes would work.

When considering applying the highest level of control, such as replacing actions of people with technology, the most complex consideration is how people will react to the change and how will the change impact them. The best outcomes are achieved when your employees know what their future holds. Values-driven leadership is essential to successfully engage employees when undertaking a change of this nature.

The automation of a process can be expensive, and the manager must be certain that the activity being automated cannot be managed in another way. The manager should have a high degree of confidence that the application of technology is:

- Required
- Creates significant value
- Has the right commitment from people to find the best solution
- Is a strategic priority

Developing new technology is often expensive and carries unknowns that may be difficult to quantify. In most cases, being a fast follower (waiting until someone else has ironed out the unknowns) is the most cost-effective strategy. The exception is when the improvement relates to a high-value

leverage process in the business and if you have already established a level of maturity in operational excellence.

If an organisation precludes taking any risk on new technology it's likely it's wasting a capability that exists within the organisation, and it may be leaving the door wide open for a more enterprising organisation to take its place.

It is often said that it takes at least three points of confirmation before a person translates information into meaningful action. This principle must be incorporated into every aspect of how the organisation implements projects that require behavioural change.

It is not sufficient to hold a workshop about a change initiative and then expect this to translate into action. At every step, what the leadership focuses on and acts upon is critical. Results will in most cases be proportional to the effort applied.

Example:

In an organisation looking to eliminate all injuries in the workplace the senior management made repeated pleas to the workforce to prioritise safety above all else.

Employees were required to attend behavioural training workshops. Scoreboards were erected to alert them of incidents and injuries. Performance payments were linked to safety outcomes and regular safety meetings were established.

After these initiatives, the overall safety performance did not statistically improve. How can this be? On evaluation of the standard work of leaders, it was found that less than 10% of leaders' time was being devoted to safety improvement.

This statistic is very telling. It means that the leadership was pre-occupied with more important matters. Equally, it is uncommon to find an organisation not performing well in safety when the leadership can verify that over 15% of their time is being allocated to safety.

In winning organisations, effective leaders demonstrating this characteristic will have:

- A clear understanding of the role of leaders in improving performance
- Leaders who accept their accountability for the performance of their team
- A focus on teamwork and clarity around behavioural expectations

11. Develops standard work routines

Winning organisations continually seek to minimise harmful variations. Standardisation of routine work provides a stable base to be able to improve from and an efficient way to organise communications and decision-making.

Standard work includes meetings, work procedures and schedules for when routine tasks are to be executed. This helps leaders tie together the way the organisation functions.

The drive to establish effective standard work routines must come from the leadership of the organisation. Leaders must be committed and disciplined in how they allocate their time.

Standard work routines are an important part of lean thinking as they ensure that the work is aligned to the value stream processes and that communication, planning and decision-making are organised. This reduces waste and helps ensure communications are shared and aligned.

Example:

In a large construction site one of the goals was for zero harm to people working on the site. As part of the approach to safety management, personnel were encouraged to go into the field and observe and interact with people regarding safety.

After a month, the number of people participating in reviews began to drop off and the attendance of senior managers dropped off completely. Contributing to the attendance drop off were management meetings called at short notice that clashed that were deemed compulsory.

The lack of incorporating the safety work into the standard work routine for the site de-prioritised it. Building the safety work and management meetings into the monthly schedule resolved the attendance problem and this helped this site achieve best-in-class safety performance.

In winning organisations, effective leaders demonstrating this characteristic will have:

- Standard work routines for the organisation
- Aligned role responsibilities to the standard work required to support work management systems
- Communication boards or similar for each work area which are used to communicate and track critical actions
- Planned where they allocate their time to ensure that people influencing work is a priority

12. Utilises planning processes based on valid data to determine the critical few priority actions

Winning organisations understand that work that is planned is much more productive than un-planned work.

It is the work of leadership to establish effective planning systems to identify and prioritise where resources are allocated. Tracking and reviewing the effectiveness of planning systems allows the organisation to learn and improve.

Winning organisations understand that becoming better, faster and cheaper at delivering value requires effective planning.

Effective planning helps find the efficient way to achieve this. Identifying and then executing the highest value opportunities is key; this creates more value in a given time with fewer resources.

Any organisation's rate of improvement is affected by how well they can measure and understand their processes, capture and analyse improvement opportunities, and prioritise and allocate the right resources to the right work at the right time.

An organisation must capture the ideas and knowledge that exists from internal and external sources before it can achieve the highest rate of return from assets. The ideal situation for a leader is to have access to all the possible improvement opportunities. Focused improvement is achieved when a deep portfolio of ideas and potential projects is created and supported by careful analysis to decide on the highest value opportunities. Employees must understand how they can contribute their ideas for improvement.

The discipline to ensure that work is planned and then executed to plan can sometimes be perceived as restricting innovation. However, it is only through disciplined planning and disciplined execution of the critical few projects that a winning organisation can be achieved.

Example:

In a manufacturing organisation, a supervisor expressed his disappointment that the idea he had submitted to the engineering department months earlier had not progressed. He was disillusioned about the commitment of managers to improving the process and had become demotivated.

Upon review, it was clear that many suggestions for improvement were being submitted and few were proceeding to action. The process for reviewing

improvement ideas was not well designed. The ideas were written onto a form and then ushered around a list of people for review and sign-off. There was no feedback process and tracking was difficult.

The process was redesigned to include the ability to see the projects, their status and the ability to track progress. Several of the review steps could be done in parallel in the redesigned system. This allowed for accelerated analysis and improved choice of projects for execution.

The new system improved the understanding of the process, improved communication on what was going on which then improved the acceptance of the importance of idea submission and the discipline of selecting the highest value projects for execution.

Effective planning is the essential work of management in winning organisations. A passion for effective planning comes from understanding that planned work is typically more than three times more productive than unplanned work. A high level of planned work will deliver a high level of efficient execution.

Example:

As part of an executive training course a simple exercise was assigned to teams of five to six people. They were asked to disassemble a box containing six bent tubes that protruded through dedicated holes in the box. Then they were to transport the materials and each team member through a hoop before reassembling the box. There were some important details to understand regarding tube position, hole allocation and sequence to be able to efficiently put the box back together again.

When asked to estimate how long it would take to complete the task, typical estimates were 15–20 minutes. After a first attempt, some teams were unable to put the box back together. The best time was 30 minutes.

Progressively, over four attempts that involved developing a written plan, clear role accountability, practice and learning, assigning of clear tasks, discipline and effective social processes to engage each team member, the time to complete the task was consistently under 30 seconds.

This experience profoundly illustrated to participants how well-planned and executed work is more productive and more rewarding. The participants also learnt that an upfront investment in planning is a required and important step to achieving a winning result.

Providing a written plan to subsequent new teams eliminated cases where the team could not re-assemble the box, however, several attempts were still required to approach the 30 second level of performance. This highlighted the importance of clear task assignment and practice, no amount of reading about doing a task can substitute the value from actually doing a task.

Example:

Someone needed to replace a section of piping in a milling plant. When the job is done with two tradesmen and the correct parts, the job took three hours to complete.

On this occasion, two tradesmen were assigned to the job. When they arrived, the required parts were not available. So, they went to find the parts. When they returned the operating team had gone for morning tea, so they could not get the permissions required to commence the work.

After morning tea one of the tradesmen was called to another urgent job. The single tradesman continued. There were components of the job that could not be done in the same way with one person. The single tradesman had to devise improvised slings to handle the pipe section, creating greater risk of injury.

The job wasn't completed before the end of the shift and had to be finished the following day. That section of the plant was unable to operate in its incomplete state until the job was completed.

In this example, a job that, if executed as it was planned, would have taken three hours. Instead it took 16 hours and incurred an additional 20 hours' downtime for operations. This type of scenario is all too common in organisations where there is a weak commitment and capability to plan work and execute it according to the plan.

In winning organisations, effective leaders demonstrating this characteristic will have:

- A clear commitment to effective planning
- The discipline to analyse and prioritise opportunities
- The capability to evaluate value and allocate resources to priority opportunities
- A pipeline or portfolio of opportunities to choose from
- The discipline to focus on executing the small number of highest leverage projects at one time

13. Assigns clear tasks and regularly reviews progress

The leadership in winning organisations understands that errors can occur in communication and consequently, are committed to their work of assigning clear tasks.

Review is a critical action where errors or unforeseen aspects of tasks can be identified and plans modified if required. All tasks require a common understanding of what needs to be done by whom, with what and by when. Tasks need to be accepted by the person accountable for doing the work to achieve best results. Some form of written definition of tasks is required that specifies how performance will be measured.

A key question in every engagement survey relates to how clearly the employee understands the tasks for which they are held to account. Ensuring that tasks are clearly assigned is a key component of the leadership process. Leaders make decisions on task assignment, monitor task execution and review progress to ensure that the team is on track to achieve its overall objective.

The CPQQRTP (Macdonald) and SMART (George T Doran) Models provide useful reference guides for achieving clear task assignment.

Clear task assignment

We all can remember a time when we misunderstood a request or direction and the emotional response of feeling unfairly judged for something that was not our fault. For judgement of performance to be fair, the person must understand clearly what they are required to do and must accept that they will undertake the task as specified by the person assigning it (the customer).

To avoid the practical and emotional repercussions that are certain to occur if tasks are not completed, winning organisations always seek to clearly define critical tasks and ensure that they're accepted by the person accountable for action. There are at least two useful models for task assignment:

- CPQQRTP
  - Context—Where this task sits in relation to the bigger picture
  - Purpose—Clear statement detailing what outcome the task must achieve
  - Quantity—Statement detailing how much output is required
  - Quality—Statement detailing the specifications for the output
  - Resource—Statement of what resources are available to complete the task

- o Timeliness—The timeframe in which the tasks must be completed
- o Performance dimension—If the person could exercise discretion to improve the output, in which area would the customer prefer? For example: fewer resources, finish earlier than requested or higher quality.
- SMART
  - o Specific—Clear outline of what needs to be produced
  - o Measurable—Defines how outcomes will be measured
  - o Achievable—Person doing the task must accept that they can meet the expectations of the customer
  - o Relevant—The resources available, linkage to the plan, contextual fit
  - o Time-bounded—Defines when the task can start and when it must be completed

Tasks cannot be assigned to a person without him/her accepting the task. Acceptance is an important part of achieving alignment on what is required and the boundary limits.

It's important for the person assigning the task because it increases the chances of getting the output desired and it's important for the person executing the task as they need to understand what it is they are required to produce and to decide whether they can do it. How performance will be measured provides the clarity needed to understand the value required to complete the task and establishes the basis for a fair assessment of performance.

Some level of written task assignment is essential to build a robust understanding of what is required to assign clear tasks.

Even complex tasks can usually be adequately defined on one to three pages of type written text. It is ironic how much is written into legal contracts about consequence and redress associated with dispute or lack of performance, and how little is written about the work itself. Getting the task definition clearly written, commonly understood and accepted by the sponsor and the person responsible for executing it, not only will ensure a greater chance of success, but also a reduced likelihood of needing the redress clauses.

In winning organisations, effective leaders demonstrating this characteristic will have:

- Written key tasks assigned to their employees that are clearly defined and accepted by the accountable person
- Regular and meaningful progress reviews of key tasks occurring
- A fair basis for assessing performance in the execution of key tasks
- Employees who feel that they clearly understand what is required of them and that they have the resources required to execute their work

14. Analyses the degree to which work is executed to the plan

Leaders in winning organisations understand that nothing can be assumed with certainty. It is essential to analyse how well the organisation can complete tasks as they are planned to learn and improve performance.

There will always be opportunities to improve planning and execution of plans. If you track the progress in executing planned tasks, you'll almost certainly discover that the outcomes achieved do not perfectly match planned estimates. Some outcomes will be better and some will be worse than estimated.

It is important to remember that the actions chosen were those that had been identified as creating the most value. Identifying the causes for variation in outcomes is an important input into the planning process to support improvement.

Example:

The piping meters that were being installed in a construction project were behind schedule. The causes for this were attributed to underestimating the time it took to refurbish some older pipes, lower labour productivity and weather delays. The manager needed to get back on schedule, however, the extra time required for refurbishment could not be reduced. The analysis of productivity also did not reveal any significant opportunity. The best opportunity identified was to reduce the impact of weather. Other jobs could be continued in wet weather, so the manager increased the labour allocation to piping when the weather was fine and moved the labour to other work when it was wet. Combining the work of different groups required significant communication and negotiation to ensure that the overall project schedule could be achieved. By following a detailed plan and tracking execution progress in a timely manner, the team could make an early intervention to address harmful variation.

In winning organisations, effective leaders demonstrating this characteristic will have:

- Measures of how well work is being executed
- A sound understanding of planning effectiveness
- Leadership engagement in review of work execution
- Learnings from work execution that are captured and available to improve planning

15. Knowledge management systems are owned by senior leadership to develop ASK-LEARN-SHARE behaviour throughout the organisation

Winning organisations require effective knowledge management systems to ensure that all employees have access to the best information required to support sound decisions.

Ideally, everyone's knowledge should be available to be shared when it is required. To achieve this, you need a culture that values sharing knowledge. Your team should be able to collaborate in seeking to ask questions, learn from others and share their own knowledge.

The governance of knowledge management within the organisation must be owned at the top. Senior leadership must recognise, reward and demonstrate the behaviours of ASK-LEARN-SHARE (Reference: Royal Dutch Shell Ltd).

The objective of knowledge management is to ensure that every employee can access all the knowledge required to do their work within seconds.

When perfectly executed, knowledge management connects people to the knowledge in a way that feels seamless; every question that occurs in your head is answered quickly. The complexity of having to work out the answers to problems gives way to the simplicity of following a process. It helps limit people 're-inventing the wheel', thus saving the effort of solving the same problems again and again. Building a common or shared understanding of how people work together frees up enormous capacity and resources.

The prize of giving people the right information at the right time does not come free. The most important way to achieve excellent knowledge management is through developing a culture that values collaborative behaviour.

Collaboration is defined as people working together to achieve a shared goal. The shared goal is what matters most and the people commit to the behaviours required to achieve it. These behaviours are centred on the core values and effective communication.

The people in a collaborative organisation must see the value in taking their new knowledge and sharing it with others.

They need to practice behaviours of:

- ASK—when a problem or question arises, the person's first assumption is that this has occurred before and someone knows a solution. His/her

work is then to find the answer.

- LEARN—once the information arrives the person needs to assimilate it, understand it and learn how to use it
- SHARE—now that the person has taken what was known and made use of it, he/she then makes the effort to add any key learning into the common knowledge database for future reference by others

The internet provides a powerful tool to connect people to knowledge. However, not all the available information is of the same value. The challenge for any knowledge management system is to ensure that the 'best knowledge' is easily found. The power of the search facility and how the information is tagged, stored and retrieved is an important thing to consider in the design of any system.

It takes work and time to build an effective knowledge management culture within any organisation. Experience has consistently shown that growing the participation in knowledge sharing requires constant prodding by an influential champion.

Even with an effective champion, growing the participation level is difficult. Participation growth is linear rather than logarithmic. Building a collaborative culture requires the regular attention of a champion and must be a cultural imperative demonstrated to employees by the senior leadership. The champion must ensure that content is relevant, with new material being added to maintain the interest of the participating community.

People building knowledge management capability often raise the question of how to ensure the quality of information in the system. Most organisations find that concerns of garbage in, garbage out is less of an issue than some might think. It is the SHARE habit that ensures the quality aspect is controlled. Ensuring all contributions are transparent and traceable to the person who posted it has proven to be an effective control on quality.

Best practice transfer vs knowledge of what is achievable

A common phrase used in business is 'transferring best practices'. This often translates into a senior manager seeing a way of doing something in one location and sending leaders from another location to learn and adopt it.

This sounds like a good approach. However, often there is much inertia in transferring a method from one organisation to another. Attempting to transfer a method without understanding why can result in a low level of ownership and energy to support the change. It is always better to allow people the

opportunity to learn about the better achievement and then allow them to find the pathway most suited to their organisation and their circumstance. Ownership is an important factor in the success of adopting best practice. The important work of leaders is to define what is required and challenge the people to work out how best to achieve as good or better performance.

The problem of focusing on transferring the method can be that simply adopting a method without understanding the supporting theory is unlikely to deliver the results.

Often Lean Six Sigma implementations fail because the focus is on learning the methods. Yet these methods are less effective when they're bolted onto an organisation rather than built into the way it operates. Trying to implement something as simple as the Toyota 5S approach to workplace organisation is much more successful when people respectfully learn about 'what has been done' and they understand the supporting theory. Allowing people to then translate the approach into their culture, their language and their circumstance builds ownership and increases the likelihood of success.

The internet and collective learning

The development of the internet and the speed in which people can find information has seen the emergence of more collaborative problem solving or collective learning.

Before the internet, people with a problem to solve would typically set about solving it themselves. Now people with a problem seek to find the solution via the internet; the first response to a problem is the assumption that someone else has already solved it.

Winning organisations need to build networks that allow people to get the right information at the right time. The information systems must aspire to build collaborative networks. You should avoid organisational structures that may lead to the concentration of knowledge and power to a few expert people.

All roles should have 'knowledge sharing' as a required behaviour. People who seek to use knowledge to increase their power have no place in a winning organisation. Winning organisations value collaborative, team-oriented behaviours and place importance on recognising the effort of employees in sharing and learning.

In designing an organisation, the designers need to consider, 'How will knowledge be shared?' For example, in highly-centralised organisations such as traditional universities or research departments, people can lose touch with changes outside of the institution unless specific interactions with industry groups and student groups are designed into roles and governance processes.

The prevalence of social media in the lives of so many today, creates great learning, sharing and influencing opportunities. Winning organisations must incorporate the use of existing digital media platforms as part of finding the most cost-effective solutions for customers. There is significant power and cost-effectiveness in using digital platforms to communicate and build new ideology-based organisations.

Today, there are large informal organisations using internet forums to communicate which can mobilise people into action anywhere in the world. An idea can quickly reach millions of people in seconds. Unlike any time before, millions of people have almost constant connectivity with their social network.

Conventional organisations are required to be legally accountable to their stakeholders including employees, communities and customers. Local laws and standards have been developed to hold organisations to account for their activities according to the standards and rules of that community.

Today, conventional organisations are being challenged by incredibly low overhead web-based businesses that instantly have a global reach. These network-based organisations provide the platform for customers to connect to individual service providers. The owner of the platform makes profit from high-volume low-cost fees as customers find suppliers in an online marketplace.

By avoiding the accountability and overhead costs of conventional organisations, the customer accepts higher risk to achieve a much lower cost for products or services. The power to provide global feedback of customer satisfaction mitigates the risk significantly, as suppliers are acutely aware that if they don't deliver on customer expectations they may quickly be out of business.

These types of organisations are growing in many areas, including financial services, commuting, home care, asset swaps and home maintenance. They are likely to challenge conventional organisations to an increasing level. How local laws and standards become applied to these new ways of doing things will take some time to work out.

At the end of the day, these organisations challenge the value being generated by all the management and hard assets in conventional organisations. If the customer can get as good or better service from connecting with individuals for much lower cost, this is what they will choose. You can be assured that the individual supplying the service understands that their success is largely in their own hands. The felt accountability and ownership of their work in meeting the customers' needs is crystal clear when it is easy for a dissatisfied customer to inform all future customers of their experience.

Franchising is an organisational model that has proven successful. Franchising thrives in traditionally fragmented but lucrative sectors by providing a consistent recognisable and desirable product or service. The franchise organisation provides the systems, the training, the expertise, the logistics and the development of the brand. The franchisee invests significant capital with an expectation that they will be in control of their own destiny; that they will be business owners. Having a capable and engaged franchisee who can follow the proven recipe is what the franchisor is seeking.

The franchisor is seeking to achieve a winning organisation as the means to grow market share and entice the right franchisees who want to invest.

Today there is no doubt that winning organisations need to increasingly utilise digital media as part of their operating strategy. Already analytics and neural networks are cost effectively mining the internet data that is available to increase the reach and effectiveness of finding and influencing customers to increase market penetration.

Value Focus

Figure 8: Winning Organisation Model's value focus characteristics

CUSTOMER

16. Specifications for all products and services are clearly defined
17. Voice of the customer is incorporated into improve processes via regular formal feedback processes

PLANNING

18. Market intelligence and competitor analysis is conducted that considers: supply and demand, cost effectiveness, quality and potential for substitution and business changing innovations
19. A plan exists that defines how the organisation will ensure that the right people with the right skills are doing the right work in the right way to achieve the vision
20. The degree to which tasks are executed according to plan is measured and a focus for improvement
21. Planning estimates the level of risk (or confidence) of achieving a given performance output
22. Planning process includes top down and bottom up verification process to achieve alignment and the critical tasks required to achieve goals
23. No work can proceed without the approval of the budget owner
24. A financial model built upon process drivers is used to analyse and estimate the value of opportunities
25. The financial model considers the life expectancy for critical assets of the organisation

ANALYSING

26. A structured method is established to capture, analyse and improve ideas as an input to planning
27. Process simulation is used to understand the impact of interactive variation and bottlenecks when considering high cost interventions
28. Discipline exists for improvement ideas to be subject to a valid cost benefit analysis as part of determining priorities

Value focus is one of the four essential capabilities in WOM. Every effort that does not create value is waste. All organisations have waste and only those that can minimise it and keep delivering value more effectively, faster and cheaper than the competition will sustain a best-in-class performance.

Value focus capability requires a clear understanding of the purpose or value proposition of the organisation. A winning organisation must develop the capability to analyse opportunities and plan the best pathway to meet those goals with acceptable limits. Value focus requires a relentless discipline to critically assess the value proposition of every action and to seek improvement through allocating scarce resources to the few highest value projects.

Value focus capability must be agile so that the organisation can act in a timely manner. Time is an important resource. Most organisations will improve over time. However, if the rate of improvement is too slow, then the organisation will lose out to more agile competitors.

Value focus capability requires a balance of risk and reward in deciding when a project is ready to move into the execution stage. It also needs to have the authority distributed down through the organisation so that initiative and time is not wasted by layers of review.

Winning organisations have established a pipeline of potential projects that may be at various stages of definition and readiness. Having a pipeline of ready projects is required to sustain high rates of improvement.

Customer

No customer = no business.

There is no shortage of ideas in the world. However, it is only when someone is willing to pay for value created that there is potential for an idea to have commercial value. Even when customers are willing to pay for it there needs

to be enough demand, at a sufficiently attractive margin, before investment should be committed. Any Investment where the return on is negative or less than other alternatives options is destroying value.

It is unwise to commit resources to any idea, however good it seems, without first testing whether there are customers who are willing to pay a suitable margin above the cost to deliver the service or product. The notion of committing resources and then trying to attract customers is a folly that is more likely to result in poor financial outcomes

Validating that there is a market before investing capital, and preferably securing commitments with customers to buy the product or service, increases the confidence level of any value estimate.

Quality is one of the minimum suite of measures required to understand a process. Quality is commonly associated with products that are well made or better than other similar products.

The idea that customers should pay more for quality has long been used in marketing. Quality is providing the customer output that is within the specification they paid for. If the customer is paying for product features that they do not want or need this destroys value.

The specified limits included in quality should include:

- How much?
- By when?
- By what method?
- At what cost?
- With what functionality?
- As measured by?
- How will customer feedback be received?

The minimum objective is to provide the customer with the value they have paid for. Understandably, suppliers like to delight their customers by providing additional value that the customer did not have to pay for. This may help positively differentiate the supplier in the marketplace. However, the supplier organisation must not commit additional resources to delighting the customer as this would be reducing margin.

By understanding the customer's needs, the supplier will understand how to exercise discretion in ways that create additional value to the customer without incurring additional cost.

Example:

> *A customer was paying for steel fabrications to be refurbished within one week. The refurbishing company found that they could complete the turnaround within three days instead of a week.*
>
> *They could have done nothing and simply held the refurbished items until the end of the week. However, in discussions with the customer, they discovered that the shorter timeframe was highly valuable to them, more so than a possible cost reduction. In this case the refurbished items were on the critical time path in a large plant shutdown that was most sensitive to the time that the plant was down.*
>
> *This led to a new supply arrangement with greater value being placed on shorter turnaround times. The supplier benefited by building a more trusted relationship, being offered more work and building a competitive advantage from a reputation of working with the customer to achieve better outcomes.*

Central to value focus is finding ways to deliver the value that customers pay for more effectively, faster and cheaper.

16. Specifications for all products and services are clearly defined

Achieving the least variation in processes used to create value requires low variability from input products and services. It's essential to define specifications, whether they be internal or external. Specifications must be matched to the specified outputs of each process.

Winning organisations understand that there must be cost-benefit considerations in setting specifications. It is wasteful to impose higher quality specifications than required to produce a product.

Example:

A nickel plating refinery suddenly had a problem with the surface finish on the plated sheets. A review of all normal causes revealed nothing.

Working from theory, the team established that something was impacting the surface tension of the plating solution. Eventually, the contaminant was traced to oil in the soda ash bath additive used to control pH. This oil was present in varying degrees in the ground from where the soda ash was extracted.

Oil was not something that either the supplier or customer ever thought to measure (the product specification was for 99% pure soda ash). No one had ever thought that oil could be a significant impurity in the remaining 1%.

For this reason, power stations in Japan will not purchase coal based upon a laboratory specification sheet alone, as they know there could be other variables not measured that may impact how the coal performs in their plants. They require a trial of any new coal source, in addition to acceptable lab specifications, before passing the product as suitable for general supply.

Example:

A new online auction process was introduced into an organisation to get the best price for an item. The specification of a spare pump listed in the site store was placed into the auction.

Much to the pleasure of the procurement team, the auction delivered approximately a 30% saving for the spare pump. However, when the spare pump was taken to be used in a maintenance job, a problem became evident. It was a bare pump and as such, was m

issing the fittings that had previously been supplied as part of the pump. This was discovered by the maintenance technician when he went to change out the pump. Unfortunately, the job had to be put on hold until the fittings could be sourced which created was and loss of performance of the production process.

Even though the pump specification was correct, the new auction process forced the supplier to strip back the extras that had normally been supplied to win the order. The cutbacks also extended to dropping the after sales support.

Getting the inputs at the right quality, in the right quantity and at the right time is fundamental to being able to execute work as efficiently as possible. Online auctions have become a popular tool in procurement today to ensure that competitive reverse auctions deliver the best price for a service or item. Sometimes the customer does not know what they truly value until they notice it has gone. This can be a pitfall of online auctions or simply buying the cheapest items from a specification sheet.

Example:

A raw material added to electrolytic aluminium smelting cells was sourced from a new supplier at a fraction of the usual price. The specification for the replacement looked in a similar range, except for the bulk density, which was not normally considered important.

The new product had a very low bulk density which impacted the ability to add the material into the process. It was a bit like swallowing a pill every day, except with the density change, the pill was now equivalent to the size of a pillow. The specification was updated and the same mistake was never repeated.

Winning organisations require effort in defining and acquiring the right input materials and services. They also ensure that any variability is within the limits required for the 'in-process' transformation or transportation and within the corresponding output limits required by the customer.

Example:

In an established mining operation, the management focus was on digging ore out of the ground at the lowest cost. This cost was often driven by volume and grade (percentage of metal in the ore) considerations. The unwanted impurities in the ore were removed in subsequent concentrating

and refining process to make a saleable product.

Refining processes are designed to process ore within certain grade limits. Over time, increases in certain impurities within the ore created the need for a significant investment in additional refining steps to deal with this impurity problem.

If the impact of the impurities had been fully considered in decisions on mining sequence, the blending of ore to keep the impurity below the refining limit would have enabled a more cost-effective solution. In this case the problem was not taking a full end-to-end view of the process in production throughput planning so that cumulative impacts of higher impurities were not recognised.

17. Voice of the customer is incorporated to improve processes via regular formal feedback processes

What is valued by today's customer will not be enough for future customers. Winning organisations seek to incorporate customer feedback to improve processes. What customers value needs to be continually tested and factored into the improvement, planning and prioritisation processes.

In the eyes of the customer, it is necessary but not sufficient for process output measures to be used to determine the performance of the organisation. Incorporating regular face-to-face feedback is critical to understanding the changing mood or expectations of customer representatives or advocate groups.

Communications should include perspectives from customer representatives, management and from the people using the product. There is often a gradual breakdown in the perceptions of the customers toward a product or service before it is reflected in buying habits.

However, once the customer has changed their perception of a product, supplier or brand, it can be almost impossible to attract them back.

Example:

A remote mining camp was experiencing negative feedback regarding the quality, variety and in some cases, quantity of food.

The camp manager's first response was to defend the service as being within the limits of the agreed contract. This was not a response likely to change the perceptions of the people giving the negative feedback.

The management considered the people in the camp to be privileged to be able to work and live at the site; they did not consider them as customers. The people, however, felt that they were being treated disrespectfully by the management.

A new clear vision for the management was created. It identified that its purpose was to provide the best camp experience for their guests within budget limitations. Once the management adopted the new objective, the perspective on how they viewed the people in the camp changed from privileged malcontents to valued guests and customers. Then relationships began to improve. Importantly, the vision was proudly shared with the guests.

One positive initiative was led by the head chef, who commenced routine discussions with customers asking how they enjoyed their meal and what suggestions they could offer for improvement. By having face-to-face regular communication and listening to the customers' suggestions, the chef built a respectful relationship and established a mutual shared commitment to improve. The customer felt valued, was being listened to and was involved and consequently, felt some ownership in the decisions or actions taken.

Whether the food was any better from a technical health perspective I do not know. However, the feedback became more positive and the camp went on to be recognised nationally within its parent organisation for providing excellent service.

It is essential for a supplier to incorporate customer feedback into the improvement process. The supplier and customer must establish a common and clear understanding as to how performance feedback, improvement ideas and changing expectations will be communicated and acted upon. The customer's perspective is essential in testing the relative value of ideas that may change product or service outputs.

The specification provided to the supplier can sometimes be a proxy for what is really important to the customer. When the supplier and customer work collaboratively it often leads to the discovery of new opportunities that neither party may have realised independently.

Example:

In typical export thermal coal specifications, the ash content is used as an estimate of how well the coal will perform in the emission control system of the customers' power plants. It is the chemical composition of the ash that really matters and so, for a supplier, it is very worthwhile to work with the customer in optimising coal performance.

One company identified that there was significant value to the customer in meeting emission limits by blending coal from different coal seams to optimise the sodium content of the ash. This improvement opportunity would not have been possible without including the customer in the analysis and improvement process.

Example:

> *A government organisation mandated that all new contracts would be subjected to a formal tendering process to ensure that the process was open and that best value services were assured due to competitive bidding.*
>
> *It was surprising to many that competitive bidding did not result in the expected savings. The main outcome desired was lower cost. One of the contracts involved cleaning services. The current cleaning contractor had been providing the services as requested for over 10 years.*
>
> *When the commercial manager sat down with the manager of the cleaning service and declared the objective was to reduce costs by at least 30% they decided to put a joint team together to share ideas.*
>
> *With the supplier and customer working together to transparently review how money was being spent, they could achieve the target savings. The savings were achieved by identifying where the customer was asking for greater service levels than were really required; using foam soap rather than liquid soap in washrooms, less cleaning scheduled for the more expensive night shift and reducing the amount of waste being generated by reviewing types of waste being collected were lucrative ways to reduce cost.*
>
> *The result was that the supplier's profitability and the cleaning staff's pay were not adversely affected, and the customer achieved a significant cost improvement. By building in a continuous improvement process between the supplier and the customer both organisations benefitted.*

Incorporating customer communication accountabilities into role descriptions is necessary to ensure that the voice of the customer is connected appropriately to the organisation.

18. Market intelligence and competitor analysis is conducted that considers supply and demand, cost-effectiveness, quality and potential for substitution and business-changing innovation

Winning organisations recognise that change and innovation can occur anywhere in the world at any time. It is essential to invest effort into understanding the market dynamics and learn about new technology or changing market trends to improve decision-making.

Market intelligence and competitor analysis that considers supply and demand, cost-effectiveness, quality and potential for substitution and business changing innovation is essential in winning organisations.

By studying the competition, winning organisations can learn faster and are able to understand changing market options better than their competitors. Today's innovation often becomes tomorrow's expectation. Winning organisations require the ability to learn about the market and to be able to successfully implement the best value-creating ideas wherever they occur in a timely manner.

Resources need to be allocated to market intelligence and competitor analysis. The learning gathered from intelligence must be used in planning processes. Many organisations struggle to capture the intelligence that exists within its own people, let alone what exists in the community. Clear policy, effective information systems and a culture that understands the value of knowledge sharing is essential.

Best practice organisations begin with the goal of ensuring that, in every interaction with a customer, representatives have access to a complete database of relationships, communications and the business transactions conducted. More and more effort is being committed to building sophisticated analytics that can mine the internet for specific information as an input into marketing.

Planning

Planning is the exercise of clearly defining, step by step, the best pathway to achieving an outcome or task. It is essential to have a clear understanding of what is required for effective planning.

Planning estimates the resource requirement [including timeframe] and estimates the outcome from executing the plan. All plans are based upon assumptions derived from the analysis of past information that is applied in the future.

Planners can estimate the likelihood of any single possible outcome if they understand the range of possible outcomes from any endeavour. For example, I could plan to run five kilometres. I have completed five kilometres in 25 minutes before, but it usually takes me 30 minutes and this time it took me 45 minutes. Any time between 25 minutes and 45 minutes is possible, although 30 minutes is most likely.

Work executed following a planned method is over three times more efficient than work executed without prior planning. Winning organisations require capable planning to ensure that they are using resources efficiently to achieve the best value. Planning provides the foundation to anchor learning and analyse and improve processes. Planning reduces duplication and waste.

19. A plan exists that defines how the organisation will ensure that the right people with the right skills are doing the right work in the right way to achieve the vision

For a plan to be effective, it must clearly define what needs to be done by whom, when and in what way to achieve the required outcome. All people involved in the execution of the plan need to clearly understand their role. In most cases, this means that the plan must be written down. Winning organisations develop a culture that seeks to contribute to and follow a clear plan.

It's critical to have a clear set of objectives that are measurable and achievable that is derived from the vision or purpose of the organisation. Planning works from understanding your current capability and seeks to develop a set of actions or pathway to achieving your future objectives. The planning process refers to knowledge or data on what is currently known and seeks to analyse and improve upon that base to meet the objectives within the limits defined.

All organisations have finite resources and planning seeks to utilise them as effectively as possible to achieve its objectives.

While the plan defines a pathway, it also defines who needs to do what, when and in what way. A plan is useless if it is not followed. An effective plan will provide a clear set of tasks with the planned level of resources assigned according to its defined sequence. Clear role accountability and task assignment is required to ensure that tasks will be executed as planned.

In most organisations, there will be many tasks in execution at the same time. Scheduling is an important process that interfaces between execution and planning. It involves taking a series of tasks and organising them so that each one can be completed as planned within the timeframe required.

Scheduling requires that planning specifies a timeframe within which the task must be completed by. This allows the scheduler to bring forward or push out tasks to utilise resources more effectively and to ensure that the task can be executed as planned. Scheduling is important for improving the capability of organisations to complete work required to efficiently meet objectives.

Scheduling resources takes planning into execution

The purpose of scheduling is to ensure that each task can be executed as it was planned.

A critical step in PDCA is scheduling the resource according to how the task

was planned to be executed. What is the point of planning a task if the plan is not followed? Scheduling can be complex as there is always limited time and limited resources to organise and a sequence for the best overall result.

Example:

> *In one global organisation, there was a startling revelation that the highest leverage tasks in the plan consistently had no resources allocated to them. The roles that the planner had assumed would undertake the work were never assigned that work.*
>
> *The roles assumed in planning (typically production managers), were preoccupied in managing their day-to-day processes and hence, were already fully utilised. The short-term and long-term planning processes were never reconciled.*
>
> *What might have been considered as the critical tasks for the business were merely ideas with no hope of being executed under this scenario. There was no scheduling and weak tracking of projects to determine how well plans were followed.*

Effective planning requires effective scheduling of resources. Where conflicts exist, the scheduler must go back and either change priorities, change the way the work is done or find more resource. The schedule that lays out the resource allocation needs to be a critical and transparent extension of the plan.

All tasks assigned must pass the following steps:

- Definition
- Valuation (cost vs benefit)
- A higher-value ranking when compared with other options
- The scheduling of resources with the timeframe
- Funding available from the budget phase
- Sign-off from the budget owner and the person accountable for the task

When planning a task, try to define the best way to complete it and follow a reliable sequence of steps.

The purpose of scheduling is to ensure that each task can be executed as it was planned. Scheduling work is highly iterative, as the scheduler must sequence and shuffle many tasks within a given timeframe to address conflicts and constraints that could impact their completion. The scheduling role is often under-resourced in organisations. Schedulers must negotiate across organisational boundaries to establish the true priorities and achieve the alignment required to allow the work to be executed as planned.

Winning organisations demonstrating this characteristic will have:

- A flowcharted planning process that is used to assign tasks and resources
- Clear measurable objectives as input into planning
- Standard work routines that support planning and track the plan's progress
- Clear task assignment processes to people with the skills and ability to complete the work
- Measures to estimate the degree to which work is being executed to plan
- All types of work planned and authorised using a common planning process

20. The degree to which tasks are executed according to plan is measured and a focus for improvement

Winning organisations understand that there is the risk that value will be lost during the execution stage of a task. It is important to understand the relative contribution on performance is due to plan quality and task execution. There are always opportunities to improve planning and work execution through analysis and improve processes.

Work that is well planned, not only details the work method but also what materials to use, what quality and at what time it must be completed by. Experience suggests that planned work is at least three times more efficient than unplanned work.

If you have ever worked in a maintenance or construction role it is likely that you can understand the frustration of turning up at the job only to find that the work scope is not clear, materials are missing, and halfway through the job, you are called to different job. The organisation must be committed to improving the planning processes and must have systems in place to manage work, including tracking performance. Planning systems do not need to be complex.

Example:

A small mining maintenance team working out of shipping containers in a remote desert location used a whiteboard to capture and communicate the daily and weekly plan.

The close-knit team was achieving world-class equipment uptime using what was supposedly retired, second-hand equipment. They had the advantage of high ownership, and aligned and effective teamwork. The people knew their equipment, they managed their own spares and the planning and feedback method was simple, fast and visible to the whole team.

Example:

A maintenance job required two maintenance technicians to change a damaged valve in a boiler.

Following the standard operating procedure, the job was estimated to take two hours. Initially, two maintenance technicians were assigned. However, after half an hour, one technician was called to another job. The remaining technician continued with the job, which required him to devise a new procedure that could be followed by one person. It took all day to complete the job. The overall cost, timeliness and risk in not following the standard procedure was significant.

This organisation operated with a high degree of breakdown maintenance and the management believed that they needed more technicians. After deciding to adopt a strategy to eliminate the cause of urgent breakdown work, they learnt they could achieve greater reliability at a lower cost with approximately 30% fewer technicians.

Similar issues can occur with parts and materials. Turning up to a job without the right parts is a common cause of delay and waste on job sites. Getting the inputs at the right quality, in the right quantity and at the right time is fundamental to being able to execute work as efficiently as possible.

Winning organisations understand the importance of discipline in managing work. When different outcomes are achieved from those planned, the reason could be either that the estimations were in error or that the task was not executed properly.

The leadership must measure and understand the degree to which work is being executed according to the plan. It is not necessary for the leader to assess every task, but rather a representative sample of the work. The measure required is the percentage of tasks completed within the planning specifications set.

Winning organisations demonstrating this characteristic will have:

- Measurement of planning effectiveness
- Measurement of the degree to which work is executed to plan
- Clear task assignments that include a timeframe in which the task must be completed

21. Planning estimates the level of risk (or confidence) of achieving a given performance output

Nothing in the future is ever certain; there is always a range of possible outcomes from doing anything.

Based upon what has happened in the past we are able to predict with varying degrees of certainty the likelihood of an event or result occurring again. If the system or fundamental processes were to change then our data no longer provides the same level of accuracy in predicting future outcomes.

You need to understand that processes may no longer perform as they have done in the past. To manage risk you need to understand the factors that may impact process performance and customer preferences

Risk level is estimated by considering the likelihood of a given process change and the consequences to performance of the process should the change occur. Risk can be managed with a certain level of confidence by reducing the consequences or likelihood through analysis scenarios. Airbags in cars, for example, reduce the likelihood of a fatality in a car crash. However, even with air bags some car crashes could result in a fatality.

Winning organisations seek to understand and control risk to an acceptable level as part of the planning process. When considering the worst, most likely and best outcomes from a task, organisations can identify and apply control actions that will tighten the distribution within acceptable limits.

Example:

In constructing a large chemical plant, the overall construction cost was sensitive to the amount and price of the steel purchased. Current steel prices were above long-term averages and the trend suggested further increases in price during the project due to global high demand for steel.

To mitigate this cost risk, it was decided to purchase a portion of the steel in advance and to establish a hedging arrangement that limited the impact of potential future price rises. The consequence of these actions limited the negative impacts of steel price increases, however, they also limited possible benefits from lower steel costs if the price fell. This strategy effectively neutralises the risk of variation in steel price.

Below is an example of process variability. At any given time, the process could produce any result within the range of outcomes achieved previously. By implementing actions to reduce the range of outcomes, more uniform results from the process are likely to be achieved.

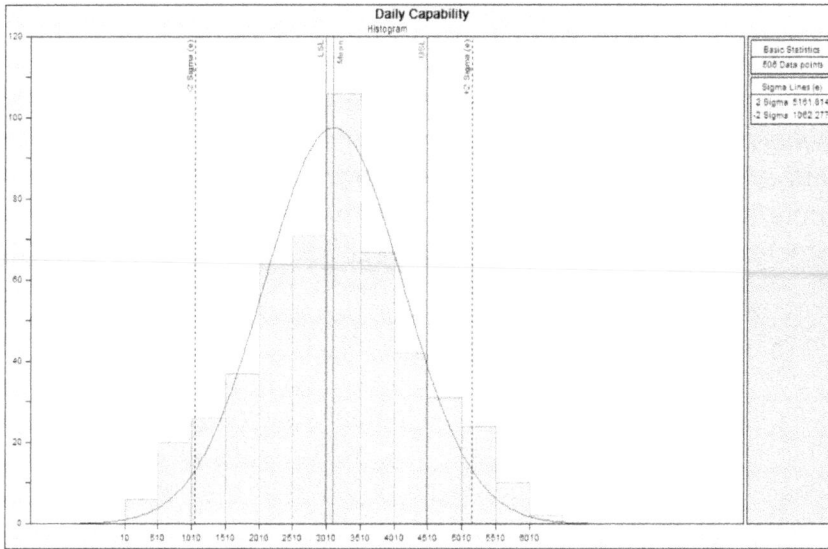

Figure 9: Process distribution chart

When presented with a run chart showing weekly mine production over a 12-month period, senior managers were asked, 'How often does the budgeted weekly production number coincide with the actual weekly production number achieved?' The answer was not very often. This prompted a discussion on why then there was an obsession with reporting whether a result was over or under-budget. The more important question was whether the process was performing within normal levels of variation.

All processes have variation and it is only by providing a probability estimate of a predicted outcome that risk can be quantitatively assessed. It's possible to achieve any data point that sits within the distribution of data from a process at any given time. For processes that have a normal distribution, the 50 percentile represents the most likely long-term average performance (provided the process remains the same).

For processes that fit a normal distribution curve the process performance can be estimated by triangulating the worst, most likely and best performance.

The average outcome is the most likely over time and has a 50% confidence level.

Monte Carlo calculations can be used to calculate the probability of a certain outcome where there are multiple variables to consider. Monte Carlo is based upon summations of 500 or 1000 iterations of accessing data points from the distribution of data to provide an estimated output.

If improvement initiatives fail to deliver the estimated benefits, the most likely cause is a lack of understanding of how changing one part of the process will impact the whole process. The most common error is assuming there are no constraints to an improvement and how it flows through the process to the final outputs. Monte Carlo calculations, when applied across the complete end-to-end process, can be useful in demonstrating the effects of variation on the process.

Business cases often don't include an understanding of the impacts of variation. Business cases often sound like, 'If we increase the capacity of the bottleneck process by 10% then we will increase the output at the end of the process by 10%.' This would only be true if the variation elsewhere in the process is small. The customer pays for the output that they receive and so all value estimates for investment should be based upon the effect on the full process through to the final outputs.

In most processes, there is variation in upstream and downstream processes that will, from time to time, constrain the performance of the process in the middle.

Example:

Process A feeds outputs into process B which produces outputs that feed into process C. Outputs from process C, are what the customer pays for.

Analysis suggests that production from B is constraining the A-B-C process. A proposal to increase the maximum production capability of B by 10% is submitted for analysis. What will be the increase in output that goes to the customer?

To answer the question, you need to estimate the impact of variation. If variation in outputs from A to B can impact the performance of B, then this must be estimated. If variation in C's readiness to take outputs from B can impact performance of B, then this needs to be estimated.

Change in final product produced (C) = change in B- (losses due to variation between A&B)- (losses due to variation between B&C)

Without understanding the impact of variation, the value from the investment will be overstated.

It can be difficult to understand the true bottleneck of a multi-stage process. It can be the cumulative variation across the full end-to-end process that is the major bottleneck.

Reducing variation across a process is, in most cases, a highly cost-effective approach to increasing the average output. Moving the average performance closer to the maximum sustainable performance (95th percentile of the process histogram) means the process is more reliable and will increase the average output.

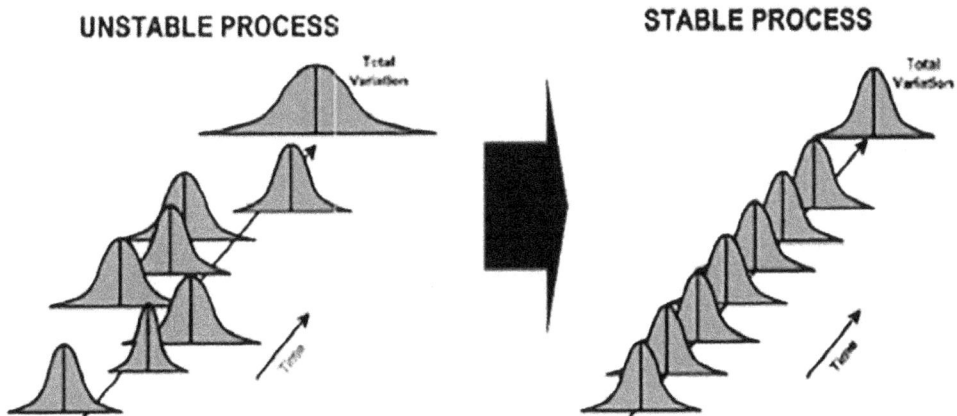

Figure 10: Cumulative Variation Chart Reference Vale Inco Asset Management Framework training materials

If an organisation seeks to consistently do what it says it will do, understanding variation is essential and planning needs to understand and put in place effective controls to deal with it.

Example:

An organisation that was focused on Overall Equipment Effectiveness (OEE) spent a significant investment to improve the availability of the fleet of trucks being deployed to move materials.

The investment delivered improvement in availability, however, it did not result in any more material being shipped from the port and hence, the return on investment expected was not realised. The reason for this was that the port operations were the true bottleneck. The result of the investment was additional trucks being parked up once the stockpile was at its maximum. The error was in not understanding constraints across the full end to end process.

In winning organisations that have long or complex end-to-end processes, planning must provide estimates of the confidence levels on planned output estimates at each stage. When planning processes contemplate variation, it is inevitable that the organisation becomes more aligned around what needs to be done to improve the process performance.

Identification of the Highest Risks from Planning

One of the minimum suite of measures required to confidently understand the performance of a process or organisation is risk. Risks are plausible scenarios that, should they occur, would significantly alter the future performance expectations of the process.

While there will always be risk, winning organisations seek to estimate it and manage their processes in a manner that controls it within acceptable limits. It is only when risk is being considered in a structured and transparent way that there can be confidence that current performance is likely to be sustainable.

Example:

A large transformer is used to supply power to a business. The business has no spare transformer and the consequence of a failure would mean weeks without full power. Some backup generators are available to provide emergency power for a prolonged period. However, no production would be possible while on the backup generators.

The transformer is aged, and based upon condition monitoring assessments, has a 20% chance of catastrophic failure within three years. Losing production for weeks would incur financial losses estimated to exceed $250,000 as well as a loss of reputation with customers.

For this business, the consequence of a transformer failure rates as a major risk. However, when applying the probability of failure, the overall risk score is below the mandatory organisation level for action. While no remedial plan is in place, the risk is included on a risk register with the action to review the risk assessment on a quarterly basis using condition monitoring data.

In this case there is no certainty that a failure will occur in the timeframe in question. It is certain that the failure will occur eventually, and it would be no surprise to anyone if the failure occurred at any time. The important consideration is that the organisation is aware of the risk and has the visibility and capability to actively manage it on an ongoing basis.

Planning must always deliver not only cost, throughput, quality and reliability estimates for outputs, but also risk estimates. It is acceptable to decide to take a greater or lesser risk in operating any processes, however, it is not acceptable to be blind to the risks that are implicit in how a process is operated. Only when risk is understood, can the process manager be confident of the sustainability of the current performance of a process.

Risk is one of the minimum sets of output measures that must be always be considered together with cost, throughput, quality and reliability to truly understand the consequences of decisions made. It is a critical component of the senior leader's role to always require that the level of risk be estimated as part of the planning process.

Winning organisations demonstrating this characteristic will have:

- Risk estimates as an essential part of planning output
- Planning estimates that detail the best, worst and most likely outcome from an action
- Value estimated on the effect the risk has on the end process step where the customer pays
- Awareness of cumulative variation effects on processes

22. Planning process includes top down and bottom up verification processes to achieve alignment on the critical tasks required to achieve goals

Effective planning requires clear objectives as an input. The planning process then seeks to find the best pathway to achieving the objective. Winning organisations verify that all levels in the organisation understand the plan and what they are required to do to ensure the overall outcomes are achieved.

The budget is an outcome of commitments made that are determined by the pathway chosen to achieve the goals set. It is only through changing the pathway (in other words the work) that the cost changes. If the chosen pathway is estimated as being over budget, the planning process needs to find another pathway through the analyse and improve process until a successful pathway is found. If no pathway can be found, then the goal itself may need to be revisited.

Some organisations spend most of their planning effort on budgeting. Setting a budget or the cost without setting throughput, quality, reliability or risk can undermine effective planning. The budget should be an outcome of estimates derived from the work required to achieve a given performance from the processes. When most of the effort is focused on setting a budget, and success is judged by being under budget, managers will resist reducing their budget year on year and when under pressure to reduce spending they will typically cut work that has a longer-term horizon. For example, the manager of a large plant is over budget, so he stops roof repairs that were budgeted for. The roof repairs were to be done over a five-year cycle. He now reports being under budget, however, if there is no consideration of the consequence of the long-term work being pushed out, being under budget may be misleading. There are many examples of this type of approach to budget management that have eventually resulted in catastrophic process failures.

Winning organisations require improvement and are less driven by whether they are under or over budget and more driven by whether the results are getting better, cheaper and faster. The improving trend is more important. Winning organisations focus on understanding how the effort or expenditure is improving the value over time.

Winning organisations understand that identifying, planning and executing the few highest value tasks drives improvement. Top down and bottom up confirmation of priority tasks builds the alignment necessary to minimise delays in execution. The faster the tasks can be completed, the faster the organisation can focus on the next highest value tasks.

In a global resource company, it was estimated that the number of man-years devoted to preparing budgets, forecasts and forecast snapshots was one hundred times more than the man-hours dedicated to executing improvement tasks. This organisation had become focused on financial governance to the detriment of effective planning to drive improvement. In this organisation, the behaviour of most managers was to secure more than enough funds to ensure that they could be under-budget for the year, as opposed to a focus on how to improve their processes to create more value.

Example:

In a large global resource company, the planning process involved each department submitting an annual budget to a corporate finance department. The corporate offices charged out their costs to each of the production units in the form of an administration overhead. The production department's focus was to produce more for less in each planning cycle.

Several months after approving the budget, corporate announced that a new performance system was to be rolled out across the organisation, including the production units. The production units had no prior knowledge of the intention to roll out a new system. However, corporate assured them that the cost of the system had been included in the administration overhead. Production unit leaders also had no knowledge of how the new system was intended to work.

It was agreed to proceed with the new system rollout. During the training on the new system, it became apparent that following the new system would require 200-man hours of additional effort for each team supervisor. The production units did not have the resources in their budget to allocate the time required to comply with the system.

The new system training was rolled out as planned by corporate and the new system was introduced. The production units failed to execute the system as designed due to their inability to allocate the managerial time required.

Corporate claimed success in introducing the new system as they had planned. Production units claimed they had executed their plan also, which did not contemplate the hours required for the new system. The result was predictably a non-compliant performance system that left employees shaking their heads. The critical issue was the failure to develop one integrated plan for the organisation that would have identified the conflicting resource demand and forced a discussion on priorities.

Building Winning Organisations

In Lean Thinking, the concept of developing a strategy on an A3-sized sheet of paper has proven to be a good way to communicate and ensure the alignment of priority tasks across the organisation

Winning organisations that demonstrate this characteristic will have:

- Standard meetings to discuss progress on priority tasks
- Alignment throughout the organisation on what the priority tasks are
- A communication board or document posted in each work area available to all employees
- Senior leaders who regularly visit work areas to listen and communicate with employees regarding priority tasks and issues

23. No work can proceed without the approval of the budget owner

Winning organisations require effective planning, prioritisation and a disciplined focus on value. The discipline to always gain the approval of the budget owner before committing resources is critical to minimising waste. Delegation of authority and budgets to those directly involved in managing the performance of a process must coincide with clear understanding by all involved of how decisions on expenditure will be made.

Not knowing who, why and when resources were committed is not consistent with efficient and value-focused organisations. There needs to be a robust linkage of organisational effectiveness culture and systems to the value focus planning and prioritising systems.

When considering committing a resource, the budget owner must ask, 'Have I budgeted for this expenditure? Is the expenditure needed? Is the expenditure needed now?' If any of these answers is no, then the budget owner needs to review the plan.

If the budget owner cannot find a solution that is within budget, then he/she needs to escalate a request to the next level of leadership. It is often the case that the next level can find a solution as they should have a broader scope and access to more resources.

Example:

In a large resource organisation, any employee could submit a request for engineering services.

Over many years, the engineering department had grown and still there were calls for more resources. Upon investigation, it was revealed that over 70% of the work that the engineering department resourced never proceeded past the scoping phase. Morale was low in the engineering department, as projects were consistently being knocked back at the execution stage.

The critical systems flaw was that the engineering team were not required to engage with the manager (final budget owner) to determine the value and priority of the work in the planning stage. The gathering of suggestions and ideas was fine, but the budget owner should have approved the allocation of resources. A change was made to ensure ideas for engineering were reviewed by the manager before resources could be allocated.

Once the planning and approval processes were aligned, the engineering department actually needed fewer resources and could achieve a higher rate of project execution due to the resources being allocated to the priority projects.

Receiving approval by the budget owner for all work before resources are committed does not mean that the business becomes bottlenecked. A competent manager will quickly identify standard jobs that are predictably required and will provide approval on an ongoing basis for these to be performed within clearly set limits.

A competent manager will break down the key tasks and assign these to other people within the team. A large budget can be broken down into smaller pieces that are managed by the right people, provided that the feedback systems are established to track performance back to an overall business plan.

In this way, the organisation becomes bound together. Whether you are the person accountable for execution or the person who has authorised the task, it is valuable to know where the boundary conditions are for your accountability.

Example:

An organisation had a major equipment rebuild that was to be executed over a weekend. Turn-around time for the task was important. All people involved understood the plan.

Once into the job, the team found that the condition of the equipment was not what was expected and consequently, significantly more work and time would be required. Knowing how important the job was, the team pushed on.

The manager turned up for work after the weekend and to his surprise, the job had taken almost double the time forecasted. The manager wished that he had been consulted as soon as the time estimate for the job had changed as he knew there were critical shipment deadlines that required things to be running as planned.

The error was in not establishing clear boundary conditions or limits that, if reached, would require a review with the manager. Providing clear limits or boundary conditions for tasks ensures people can confidently work to their ability and escalate decisions to the right people if circumstances arise that could exceed the agreed limits.

The high-level effective planning flowchart below shows the key planning steps (left-hand side) with important iterative feed processes (right-hand side).

Effective Planning Flowchart

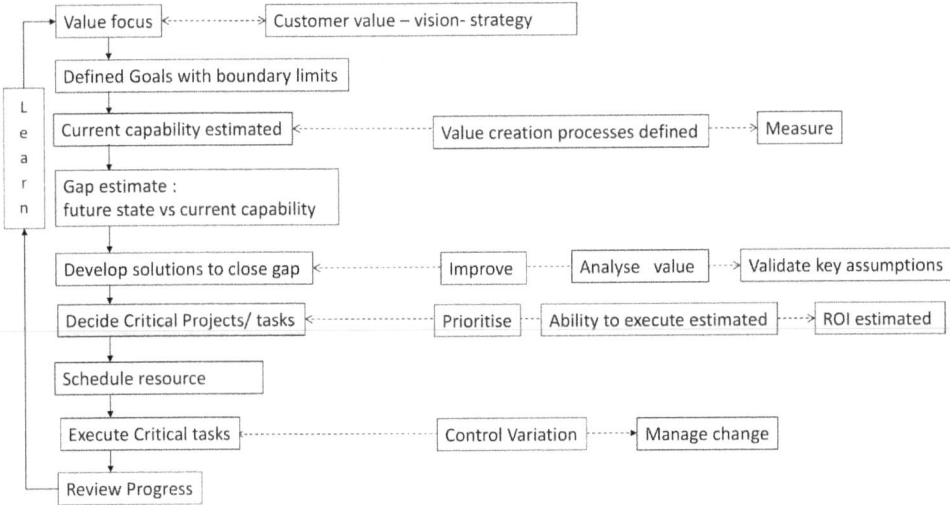

Figure 11: Effective planning flowchart

Lean Manufacturing introduced the concept of a strategy on a page to focus organisations onto the critical few high priority projects. This one-page poster-style document is displayed prominently in the workplace and is featured in standard meetings where the progress of the organisation is discussed. Strategy on a page typically defines the vision, current state, desired future state, the gap between current and future state, and the critical few actions planned to achieve the desired future state. Progress on the critical actions is updated on a weekly, monthly or quarterly basis.

It's essential to have a clear understanding of how the planning process works. The simple visual strategy on a page method of providing clarity and feedback on progress is essential.

Vision:	
3-year Goals:	
Current performance metrics:	Gap in performance to close in metrics:
Future performance metrics:	Critical tasks with updated progress report and priority actions tracked:

Figure 12: example Lay-out for a strategy on a page

Winning organisations demonstrating this characteristic will have:

- Employees who understand the planning process
- Boundary limit accountabilities and authorities that are defined, understood and complied with
- Robust controls that have been established to ensure that budget owners authorise expenditures
- Escalation processes to be used when boundary limits are reached

24. A financial model built upon process drivers is used to analyse and estimate the value of opportunities

To estimate the cost-benefit from potential initiatives, winning organisations build a financial model based upon historical process outcomes that can estimate the impacts of future scenarios. The financial model is updated and improved based on real outcomes achieved over time.

The model must be more than a profit/loss balance sheet. It must be able to link process performance, costs and value to enable reasonably accurate estimates to be determined when analysing the value proposition of improvement initiatives. These calculations are often described through value driver trees.

A simple example of mapping the value stream for a coffee making process could be as follows:

The cost of one kilogram of coffee beans at $10 makes 40 cups of coffee containing 25c worth of coffee.

A coffee machine can make 30 cups of coffee an hour with fewer than 20 minutes of cleaning every eight hours of operating. The store operates 10 hours a day so the capacity of making coffee is 285 cups per day.

Customer demand is 25 cups per hour between 7.30–9.30 and 12.00–1.30 and 4.00–5.30. For all other times, the average is five cups per hour. Current demand is 155 per day.

The cost drivers for a cup of coffee are made up of: purchase cost of the machine amortised over its life, cleaning/maintenance, labour, milk, sugar, cups, coffee and overheads. Each variable can impact the overall cost per cup and profitability. If the cost at the current average sales rate comes to $1.5 per cup and a cup of coffee is sold at $4.50 then profit estimate is $3. The model would show how with increased sales the average cost for a cup is reduced up to a point where some constraint forces a significant increase in expenditure, such as more labour or a new machine.

Having a financial model that incorporates these formulas helps the organisation focus ideas on the areas that offer the greatest leverage. In this example, it might be a priority to focus on ideas that generate demand in the quiet periods. Having established the driver calculations, the organisation can estimate the cost and benefit of changes and use the model to support planning.

Example:

In metalliferous refining, an important process objective is to convert as much of the valued metal from the ore into the final saleable product. The value stream map below was developed to assist the leaders in understanding the value of potential process improvement.

By looking at process variability, there was the potential for almost nine million dollars improvement in value if the reasons for periods of higher loss could be addressed. Prior to constructing this simple value driver tree, the organisation was unaware of the potential value that could be realised by improving this process.

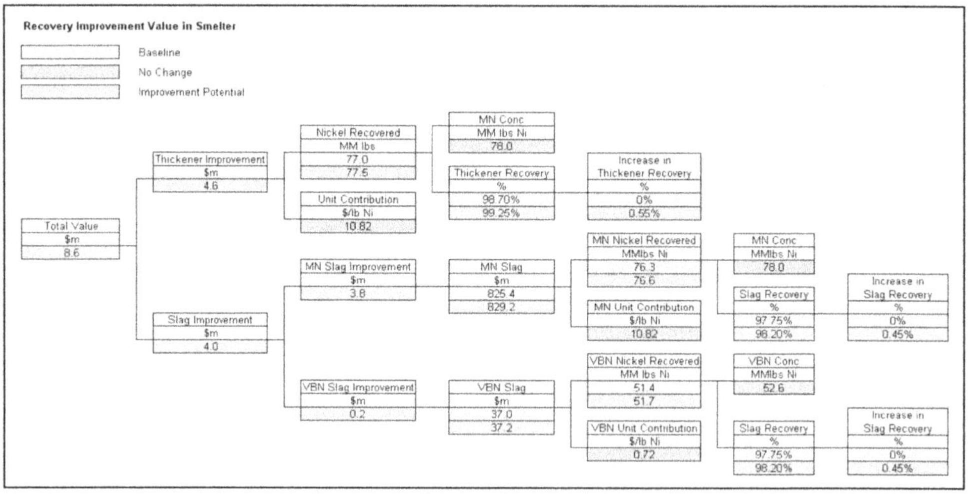

Figure 13: Vale Inco Value stream Model example

Winning organisations that demonstrate this characteristic will have:
- A simple financial model that is used to support planning that includes process driver cost value formulae
- One financial model used to identify high-value areas to focus improvement
- One financial model used to evaluate opportunities for improvement across the high-level process map (raw materials to output that the customer pays for)

25. The financial model considers the life expectancy for critical assets of the organisation

Winning organisations understand that key assets have a finite life. It is important to consider well in advance the implications of assets, resources and processes reaching the end of their economic life.

All organisations benefit from understanding what the closure or exit plan looks like. Setting a life expectancy enables the organisation to contemplate an end and in doing so, to better prepare for it.

Knowing the estimated life expectancy brings into focus consideration of options that may extend life or address the mitigating factor that limits life. The earlier that life expectancy can be considered the more time the organisation will have to create the highest value pathway.

Example:

In a manufacturing plant, the useful remaining operating life of a major transformer is five years. The estimated life of a replacement transformer is 30 years. The business itself is estimated to have a 10-year life as set by key commercial contracts.

The planning process considers its options:

1. Buy a new or used transformer and install within the next five years

2. Keep running the existing transformer to failure and as a contingency, identify a replacement option and contemplate production contingencies to cover the outage period should the failure occur

3. Downgrade the use of the transformer as a means of extending the likely life.

The planning process then compared the risk and reward from each option to decide the path forward. Without having some clear life expectancy timeframes, it would not have possible to complete the options analysis required.

There are always some closure costs for organisations at the end of life. By having a definite life built into the model that is used to analyse and set priorities the organisation can better assess the closure liability risk on an ongoing basis.

Winning organisations demonstrating this characteristic will have:
- A clear understanding of the life expectancy of key assets and the organisation
- Life expectancy considered in planning

Analysing

Winning organisations interpret and learn through the analysis of data. Analysis is a critical capability for improvement. Winning organisations understand that analysis develops new learning and provides an estimate of what might happen in the future.

Understanding the range of outcomes or the statistical certainty of an outcome informs leaders of risk and ultimately leads to actions that improve the accuracy and precision of estimates. Effective analysis requires well-designed systems that generate valid data that is captured, organised and interpreted by people to inform decision-making.

26. A structured method is established to capture, analyse and improve ideas as input into planning

Winning organisations invest in building system that facilitate data capture, analysis and project definition. When people understand how to contribute and obtain feedback and recognition they are more likely to get involved. Transparency in the decision-making process allows all people to investigate and reach a common understanding.

Ideas for improvement can occur at any time and it is important that employees know how to input their ideas into the planning process. Triggers to instigate this can include:

- The process performance moving outside of control limits
- A decision to change the process performance as part of the planning process

Central to the Six Sigma improvement method is the DMAIC process for ideas and projects.

The Six Sigma DMAIC process comprises:

Define—Clear definition of the problem and outcomes sought

Measure—Clear definition of the measures that characterise the process involved

Analyse—Review the measurement data and seek to identify cause and effect

Improve—Identify changes that will achieve the desired improvement in performance

Control—Implement the process improvements and ensure the improvements will be sustained

The Define-Measure-Analyse-Improve-Control process is a proven method that underpins the analyse and improve systems in many winning organisations. It is interesting to note that, many organisations spend most of time in the Measure-Analyse-Improve steps. Experience suggests that most of time should be devoted to Define and Control. Clarity in defining the problem to solve and effectively locking in gains with robust controls leads to faster rates of improvement.

It is unfortunate that many organisations solve the same problem many times over. This is often due to a lack of competency in locking in the improvements made. Effective controls are essential to increase the likelihood of these

improvements being sustained. Learnings need to be captured in an effective knowledge management system.

Example:

After an industrial incident in which people were killed and a plant was destroyed, investigations were made by the company, regulators, police and industry experts. From these investigations, the causes for the incident were identified and many actions and controls were recommended and implemented.

The plant later resumed operations under the new standards. Four years after recommencing operations, a former manager who had been in the organisation at the time of the fatal incident, decided, out of his personal interest in safety, to return to the plant. He wanted to review the aspects of the plant that he remembered from the incident.

What he found terrified him. He found that the practices of people had gradually deteriorated back to the way they had been just prior to the fatal incident. He felt that the same incident could likely occur within the next 12 months.

He found that no employees involved in the day-to-day management of the process even knew about the fatal incident four years earlier. It was more good fortune than good management that he had visited before the same incident reoccurred.

Without effective controls that are robustly linked to effective knowledge management, processes can drift over time, resulting in the same problems being solved over and over again.

Winning organisations require a structured and disciplined approach to how ideas are captured, defined and analysed. This is fundamental to identifying the most effective solutions and minimises the waste generated by choosing poorer options, reoccurring problems and any unwanted repercussions associated with implementing changes. A common trap in poorly defined improvement projects can be unexpected detrimental outcomes in other areas of the process. For example, increasing the octane level in fuel will give a car engine more power, however, it may lead to shortened engine life.

Ideas are the beginning of the project pipeline process. They need to be evaluated and improved upon using a common process. The progress of ideas through the project management system needs to be transparent and accountable.

Winning organisations that demonstrate this characteristic will have:

- A structured method for capturing, defining, analysing and managing ideas using the DMAIC steps
- Employees who know how to use and contribute to the planning and improvement systems
- The discipline to follow the planning and improvement system

27. Process simulation is used to understand the impact of interactive variation and bottlenecks when considering high-cost interventions

Winning organisations minimise the risk of over-investing in projects by understanding the impact of interactive variation. The value from improvements in one bottleneck area can be easily over-estimated, particularly in longer process chains.

Process simulation that contemplates the constraints and variability of processes is a cost-effective tool used by winning organisations to realistically assess the benefit of process improvements. Process simulation provides for relatively low-cost testing of improvement ideas. Process simulation models can often be built using an excel spreadsheet.

Dr Goldratt in his book *The Goal* introduced the theory of constraints, where he illustrated the importance of identifying the bottleneck or current constraint in a process and the importance of focusing improvement efforts on addressing the bottleneck. He illustrated that improvements made in areas other than the constraint are less effective in improving the output from the end of the process.

Often the constraint is not easy to identify and variation itself can be the greatest constraint in the process. Whenever we measure outputs the only variation we can see is the cumulative variation. We cannot see the contributing effects of each of the prior process steps if we only look at the end of process outputs.

Dice Simulation Exercise

A six-sided dice exercise is an effective tool to help people gain a better understanding of the impact of variation. The simulation involves looking at a process at the highest level and breaking it down into steps. Ideally you should translate the exercise to the specific process steps that best relate to the production processes of the organisation involved.

The dice can be used to reflect normal day to day variation, with the number one meaning only one unit of production and six meaning six units of production. Each dice roll represents a day's production and the performance at each step and across the whole process is tracked on a simple spreadsheet.

As in real life, each process stage can only pass on what they have produced. Assuming no stockpiles are used, if stage one only rolls a one, then even if stage two rolled a six, it could only produce one unit, as that would be all the input material that would be available.

In the exercise, each process step is assigned to a manager who reports to a general manager. There are usually CEO and business analyst roles assigned. The production of each process stage is constrained by the available inputs and the number rolled on the dice. The CEO is asked to nominate what production he/she expects the process to achieve (given the range of one to six, the average capability per step would be 3.5).

The simulation is then run for 20–30 dice rolls to generate production data. The CEO is required to review the actual production achieved and then decide what, if anything, should be changed to improve the process. Some teams focus on the bottleneck (the process stage that overall rolled the lowest numbers during the exercise), some want to spend capital to increase capacity and some want to increase inventory levels.

The perceived bottleneck in this simulation is only a short-term aberration based upon the way the numbers were rolled. Over several runs of the simulation, with the CEO choosing certain improvement options, it becomes increasingly clear that investing in more inventory or increased capacity in one or more steps does not have a significant impact on performance.

Usually, sometimes with some coaching, the option of reducing variation across the process is tested. This is done by counting a roll of one, two or three as a two, and a four, five or six as a four (thus tightening the range of possible scores from one to six to two or four).

The reduced variation makes the process becomes more predictable and the excitement from earlier stages about rolling a six or the disappointment of rolling a one disappears.

The reduction in range from one to six (average 3.5) to two or four (average 3.5) results in an increase in average production, thus illustrating the impact variation has on process performance.

You can use a simple excel spreadsheet to capture the results from rolling the dice to assess various process scenarios. This teaches participants the value of using simple simulations to test theories such as the impact of increased inventory.

Process variation can be predicted, and suitable controls applied during the process design phase. Because controls themselves will fail at some frequency, it is essential to implement sufficient layers of controls to achieve the required level of risk reduction.

In an extreme application such as in hazardous industries, organisations generally accept that the minimum level of safety acceptable in design is

less than one event in one million years. The reality is that if it can happen, it will happen. The thorough application of cause and effect analysis when systematically applied leads to new learning that can improve the predictability of a process.

For an organisation to understand and forecast performance accurately, some level of process simulation is required. Simulation models allow the impact of control changes to be tested at low cost and in an offline environment.

A simulator can provide a quantitative assessment of the probability of certain performance being achieved and can competently predict the likely performance outcomes using Monte Carlo simulation. Monte Carlo simulation requires that the range of possible outcomes for each variable be loaded into a spreadsheet. Then at least 500 calculations are completed where numbers are randomly chosen from the process distribution at each stage of the process. Collating the results of the 500+ calculations provides a much more realistic estimate of how the process will behave and can provide a valid estimate of the confidence level for the process achieving a given output.

It is possible to apply sophisticated mathematical programs that look for changing signals in the process or for statistical correlations perhaps not yet understood by the process manager. These programs, sometimes called neural networks, can be set up to operate within a control system and can reduce the risk of a person not noticing the early stages of an event.

Example:

A metalliferous refinery required chlorine gas in the refining process. A significant event occurred in the operation when a pressurised pipe supplying chlorine became blocked. The control room operator was misled by the blocked pressure gauge that indicated the pressure was normal.

The chlorine pressure gauge usually exhibited some small variation. However, once the gauge became blocked, the reading was the same every second. Background process monitoring programs can be applied that would have alerted the control room operator that a constant reading on the gauge was abnormal which would have prompted a corrective action.

In highly instrumented processes, the use of loop-tuning software can be applied to control variation without relying on a person to interpret and adjust parameters. Tuning software is relatively expensive to implement and needs ongoing expert resources to maintain. As a result, the upfront cost and time to develop the control software must be weighed against the benefits.

Gaps in planning, work execution, engagement of the workforce, skills and leadership can all undermine the effectiveness of investment in simulation and control.

Example:

In a resource-based organisation, it had been identified that the variation in power input and mass balance in a smelting process could be controlled most effectively by a computer system.

The theory was sound and the system quite simple, yet the implementation failed to deliver the results because of how people reacted to the change. The operators felt that the loss of responsibility was demeaning their capability and self-esteem. They felt that they were not respectfully consulted about the new control system change.

What the leaders did not understand was that the operators attached a high degree of self-worth to the control of furnace power. The operators sought to override the control system when it was introduced, as they felt it was necessary to minimise the dangers associated with it. They also wanted to reaffirm their importance to their management.

The leadership had been focused on solving a technical problem without adequately understanding the social aspects. Only by respectfully involving the people affected by changes in technology can leaders ensure that the final solution will be accepted.

In another department within the same organisation, employees were involved in the evaluation of options and the management of change on a much larger automation project. Acceptance and ownership of the change in this instance was high. The most important factor in its success was the clear communication about the future of employees affected by the change.

When people affected by change understand the likely future consequences for themselves, they are more likely to support it. Being involved is respectful and allows people to gain a full understanding of all the options and reasoning.

Many organisations that have sought to increase the level of computer-based control of processes have been disappointed with the results. This is almost always due to the organisation not putting sufficient effort into understanding and managing the social aspects of change.

The Importance of Seeing the Whole Process

When considering investing in a process improvement project, it is essential that the manager understands the full end-to-end process.

The effect of:

- variation
- bottlenecks
- clearly understanding the customer's needs
- understanding of supplier input variation
- understanding the underlying processes of transformation

can significantly influence the likely outcomes from investing in a change.

Example:

A well-managed aluminium business was looking to increase profits by increasing the proportion of metal allocated to high-margin slab product. The business produced several different aluminium products. On a product-by-product comparison it was clear that the slab product delivered a significantly higher margin than other products. However, when the impact of introducing more slab was evaluated using a 'whole of cast house model', rather than the station-by-station model, it was found that increased slab production reduced total plant throughput.

This learning was significant given that the casting step was the bottleneck. What had not been appreciated was: the time and metal throughput lost in alloying, furnace preparation, washing out the holding furnace between product runs, and scrap rehandling. These operations had been previously treated as an overhead for all products.

Slab cost was being underestimated as other products were absorbing some of the cost impacts. Casting slab effectively slowed down the process and reduced overall throughput. The complexity built into casting by having a diverse product range was increasing the cost of all products. A process making one product is always simpler and likely to have less waste.

The value of process simplification is often not appreciated in organisations that do not use a competent process model to assess marketing and production decisions. In the above example, when the analysis of all variables was considered, the highest margin operating scenario was to make only T-bar products. Surprisingly, the slab product offered the lowest margin due to throughput being the constraint.

It is only possible to truly test ideas and strategies using a model that considers the whole process.

It is interesting that the critical measure of performance for each shift crew was based upon tonnes of metal cast into saleable product. The best crew was the one that cast the most tonnes. The highest-rated crews would prioritise metal casting over furnace filling and metal preparation, which were not credited in the performance measure. This approach increased variation in the continuous 24/7 process. This variation also constrained overall throughput.

Understanding what was going on with metal delivery was complicated further by having two separate departments involved. Each department only understood their processes and had their own measures. It took some time before the two management structures understood each other's processes. Only when they could model the whole end-to-end process were they able to understand what was truly going on.

Measuring performance being based only on tonnes cast, also incentivised poor decision-making. Performance should always be determined across the whole process and should consider the minimum suite of measures.

Winning organisations that demonstrate this characteristic will have:

- An understanding of constraints and bottlenecks
- A whole-of-process model that can be used to conduct simulations to understand constraints and impact of variation more effectively

28. Discipline exists for improvement ideas to be subjected to a valid cost-benefit analysis as part of determining priorities

Winning organisations focus effort and resources onto the highest value opportunities. This requires a clear understanding of value, effective planning and the discipline to stay focused.

High rates of improvement are achieved when organisations focus on the critical few highest value opportunities. When the ability to prioritise is compromised, organisations tend to have many initiatives running concurrently. Too many initiatives result in under-resourcing and poor execution. Being too busy is a symptom of a poor ability to prioritise where effort is spent.

Winning organisations always have the discipline to complete a cost-benefit analysis when setting priorities. They consider the minimum set of output measures: rate, time, cost, quality, reliability and risk.

Without discipline in the analysis, planning and authorisation process, a well-intended improvement action can cause unintended noise that undermines control. The ability to manage change is essential for winning organisations. The challenge is to be efficient in decision-making, effective in communication and efficient in the execution of projects once resources have been assigned. Trying to do too many things at the same time is a common problem that results in confusion, poor task execution leading to delays and missed opportunities.

Winning organisations demonstrating this characteristic will have:

- Employees who understand and support the need for improvement ideas to be analysed and prioritised through the planning process
- Effective change management systems
- Transparent and clear feedback on where improvement ideas are in the planning process
- The discipline to prioritise resources to a few high priority opportunities

Organisational Effectiveness

Figure 14: Winning Organisation Model's organisational effectiveness characteristics

LEARNING

29. A "way we work" program delivered by leaders communicates the vision, core values, work routines and role of leaders to employees
30. Communities of Practice(CoP) are used to build solutions that are owned within the organisation

IMPROVING

31. Goals and objectives are prioritised based upon value
32. No more than 5 critical tasks at a time are assigned to a person
33. Employees have an expectation that they will be held accountable and be fairly rewarded for their work
34. Individual performance assessment is always aligned to the overall performance of the team
35. The level of effectiveness in achieving the right person in the right role at the right time is measured
36. Employee turn-over is stable and at a rate less than 10% per year
37. All employees are engaged in seeking to minimise variation, including how work is planned and executed

EXECUTING

38. The organisational design clearly describes how authority and resources are organised to achieve the vision
39. Levels of management do not exceed six, with a clear theory explaining the value of the work being done at each level
40. The number of direct reports fit within effective limits

41. All employees are provided the authority and resource required to efficiently complete their standard work
42. All roles have defined: the purpose, authorities, accountabilities, skills, relationship to other roles (vertically and horizontally) and performance outputs
43. Customer relationship accountabilities are established in role descriptions
44. Standard jobs are approved within limits by the authorised person
45. Standard work routines for the organisation (including key communication and planning meetings) are established
46. Systems are defined, flowcharted and key roles and accountabilities allocated

Winning organisations require the ability to execute the right work in the right way at the right time and with the right skills. How well you can get the right people doing the right things will determine organisational effectiveness.

People provide flexibility, creativity, intelligence and versatility. People also have the potential to become distracted, make mistakes, be motivated by non-value adding interests and may add complexity.

Winning organisations understand that people are their most valuable asset. Deriving full value from your people to create and sustain value is the goal of organisational effectiveness. People are required for executing tasks, learning and improving.

Learning

Winning organisations require the ability to learn faster than their competitors. Learning requires:

- Access to information
- A collaborative work culture
- Effective communication
- Analytical capability

Learning and innovation defines how people and systems within your organisation will improve faster than the competition. The ability to learn cannot be left to chance. Your organisation needs to have a common understanding about how to capture and share knowledge from internal and external sources. Clarity of purpose guides the priority areas for improvement that helps focus learning effort.

To become a winning organisation, the leadership needs to successfully nurture the right work at the right time by the right people and in the right way. You need to stay focused on the truly important tasks that will create the greatest value. This requires discipline and absolute certainty in identifying the goals and objectives.

Many organisations attempt more than they can effectively execute, which leads to overload, noise and confusion. A symptom of confusion often materialises when short-term urgent activities monopolise the time of leaders in place of focusing on the long-term game-changing activities.

Winning organisations require leadership that can sift through all the possible activities that could consume time and prioritise their focus on the few highest leverage items.

Example:

A Chief Operating Officer (COO) complained that answering emails was taking at least two hours per day and that there was never enough time to get the work required done. He felt like he was the bottleneck for decision-making.

The COO realised that most of the emails were a distraction with a large amount of non-important and non-urgent content. He decided to delegate the review of emails to the communications officer who also undertook the work of scheduling for the leadership team. The communication officer competently fulfilled the email review role, which freed up considerable time for the COO to focus on the priority work of his role.

Most executives who say that they are time poor, lack a clear focus or the discipline to prioritise and plan. When the executive can define and focus on the critical few high priority tasks that the organisation needs, they are more likely doing the right work of their role.

As organisations become larger and more siloed, it is common for planning processes to exist in isolation with breakdowns in the linkages to an overall strategy. Poor design of planning processes contributes to confusion, competition for resource and ultimately, the poor execution of planned tasks.

Organisations will achieve the greatest value from the resources available when they can effectively manage work priorities. The identification of these opportunities can only be achieved through the ability to learn, share, innovate and communicate effectively. This will not happen by chance; the leadership must define the importance of this way of working and be able to communicate how the organisation will manage and develop knowledge.

Example:

A science-based organisation had a long history of conducting applied research as part of its service offering to its stakeholders. At a time when cost cutting was perceived to be the most important objective, a clandestine approach to learning emerged.

Managers insisted that the organisation was no longer engaged in research and development. Employees whose roles, by design, required them to conduct at least some degree of research and development sought ways to do it without the knowledge of the managers. The result was poorly focused learning and lower rates of improvement than might have been achieved by focusing research onto high-leverage areas.

Poorly focused learning results in slower progress, waste from investing effort in areas that are not important and the disengagement of employees. How organisations learn, innovate and improve is important to all winning organisations and it is an important variable in maintaining competitiveness.

It is not only essential that winning organisations improve, it is essential that the effort of improvement is focused onto the highest leverage opportunities. To achieve this, you must invest in learning, analysis, and be disciplined in planning and execution. Knowing what the goals are, where your limits are and how you are expected to collaborate enables value creation.

29. A "way we work" program delivered by leaders communicates the vision, core values, work routines and role of leaders to employees

Winning organisations invest time and effort of senior leaders in 'way we work' programs that are part of ensuring all employees understand how to contribute their full capability.

Example:

An organisation that placed a high value on its people ran a three-day induction program that included input from existing employees and interactive team exercises. The program received consistent praise from participants who sometimes shed tears of joy from what they had learnt and from the friendships that were forged during team activities.

One middle-aged man said that the experience had changed his life. He had never met people who cared so much, or had taught him so much, about relationships and how to contribute to their organisation. This employee went on to be a successful and long-serving employee who would always take the opportunity to share what he knew with others in the team.

'Way we work' programs are an investment in people. They also provide shared learning experiences which can form the start of long-term relationships between an organisation and its people.

In effectively applying WOM, it is necessary to educate all people, as is relevant to their role, as to how the organisation intends to achieve each characteristic. Having leaders within the organisation deliver all or part of the program helps build relationships based upon common understanding and makes the program real and meaningful.

A winning organisation 'way we work' program touches on the four capabilities of value focus, operational excellence, effective leadership and organisational effectiveness. It needs to introduce the characteristics in an interactive and meaningful way.

The objective is to provide the employee with an understanding of the culture, the people, how the organisation creates value and how to seamlessly integrate and succeed as an individual and a team member.

30. Communities of Practice (CoP) are used to build solutions that are owned within the organisation

Winning organisations build ownership and collaboration. Communities of Practice (CoP) encourage people to work together to share knowledge and ideas to formulate a common solution. Winning organisations minimise duplication and maximise ownership using Communities of Practice.

People like to be successful. It's always a significant hurdle to change if you are asking someone to replace a way of doing something that they have invested their energy and reputation into. It's much more dignifying to assign a team the challenge to learn from others and find a common solution that suits your context. This invites them to find a new pathway. You are asking each participant to contribute to finding a solution.

In forming a CoP, the senior leader defines the outcome required and allows the people to 'work out the how to achieve it'. This can virtually eliminate common hurdles of acceptance to change.

Working this way helps create a respectful ask-learn-share culture. These collaborative and less hierarchical networks are often described as Communities of Practice (CoP).

The key to this approach is to clearly define the purpose of the CoP and to have a specific timeframe and clear outputs specified. By setting up a CoP in this manner, all participants come to the table feeling respected, equally important and genuinely excited about learning and contributing their knowledge to get the results required.

The use of local champions who are accountable for leading change at their site is highly effective. The champions are authorised to adopt a solution from another site or modify an existing approach to best suits their site context. Keep in mind that it is always easier to accept someone else's method when you have no method of your own. Better to ask someone how to do a job in a better way than to tell them they have been doing it all wrong.

Example:

An organisation that had previously functioned in a decentralised manner decided it wanted to develop a common best practice behaviour based safety system.

Each site had similar but different safety systems that they had developed in isolation. One site had a program called 'Stop', one had 'SLAM' and another

had 'Take 5'. The amount of emotional and physical effort invested in each program was significant. Whichever system was chosen as the one for the organisation to universally adopt, would face significant acceptance issues and cost to rebrand at the local sites that would need to change. Everything from stationery, posters, documents, training and logos on uniforms would need to change if rebranding was necessary.

The CoP needed to establish one behavioural safety program. This did not necessarily mean having to change the individual site programs completely. It was liberating for the team to explore solutions that would suit their local circumstance and meet the global need. The community quickly aligned around defining the theories, underpinning the systems required, and agreed that each site would take accountability for how to bring their local systems into compliance with the agreed universal standards and methods.

The CoP enthusiastically agreed to continue to work together to build the corporation wide approach and accepted ownership to plan their sites transition in the most cost effective and respectful way. The timeframe to achieving the centralised standard varied across sites, however, the objective of a common standard and avoidance of duplication was achieved.

The key outcome in this example was alignment around the best practice theory and the right amount of local discretion in how the theory was to be applied.

CoPs need to be authorised by the senior leader, who is accountable for its performance. Like all tasks, it must have a start and an end date. Should it be necessary to continue with a CoP, it is important to issue a new well-defined charter including objectives, timeframe and budget, as one without such clarity can become wasteful and bring the approach into disrepute.

Some might argue that anyone should be able to start a CoP as the principle is about collaboration and sharing. Without a clear shared goal, a budget and the clear and definite alignment with the priorities of the organisation, such groups are effectively unauthorised tasks and are likely to lead to waste.

Improving

Winning organisations are focused on improvement. This requires people to analyse, hypothesise and generate new ideas or theories. Role descriptions, particularly for leadership roles, need to clearly define the requirement for improvement.

The rate of improvement is dependent on the capability of the team and the ability of the leader to harness it. They must be able to engage with their team. Leaders who demonstrate behaviours that are perceived positively against the core values are more likely to access the discretionary effort required from the team.

Organisational effectiveness needs to acquire, develop and retain the people with the right skills and capability to sustain high rates of improvement. Creating the right culture, effective leadership and ways of working as a team are important considerations.

People are the drivers of improvement and effective leadership must engage, focus and improve the performance of their team in winning organisations.

31. Goals and objectives are prioritised based upon value

Winning organisations are disciplined in analysing many opportunities and prioritising the allocation of resources to the few of highest value. The process of prioritising is not always a simple one and always involves discussion and verification.

Planning is the process of identifying, quantifying and prioritising to which tasks resources will be applied to achieve the required goals and objectives.

Critical to the success of any plan is the execution of the chosen tasks at the right time with the right resources in the right way. Many organisations make the mistake of attempting too many tasks at the same time. This leads to poor execution and a poor return on effort. All key tasks need to be clearly defined and understood. In most cases, a formally written brief approved by the task sponsor and the person accountable for completing the task is required.

The Pareto Principle is a valuable tool in guiding value focus, particularly if the organisation is in a highly reactive mode. The Pareto approach enables the leadership to focus on the highest leverage areas first.

The Pareto rule is also known as the 80/20 rule because, in general, around 80% of the value (or loss of value) is being caused by around 20% of the possible causes.

The task for the manager is to find and tackle the few causes having the biggest impact. Once one cause is addressed, the team moves onto the next. By systematically adopting this approach over time, the team will have achieved a greater rate of return from their effort.

Example:

A large resource company developed a best-in-class Lean Six Sigma Program. One of the key metrics was the number of people trained to various levels of competency in the program (up to Master Black Belt).

The program used the rigorous methods of Six Sigma to define and track projects. It reported hundreds of millions of dollars in benefits in the first three years. Benefits were estimated by adding up the total value delivered from all the projects that had been successfully completed.

The bottom line outputs for the organisation did not, however, reflect the degree of improvement that was estimated. The question was raised, 'Why isn't the value being translated to the bottom line output measures of the business?'

It was identified that bottlenecks elsewhere in the process had been limiting the estimated value. The planning processes were not identifying the right projects, the focus needed to be on relieving the bottlenecks.

Many Lean Six Sigma efforts focus on so-called 'low hanging fruit' or easy win projects as an effective way to build momentum and develop belief and capability. This has some merit, if it is not prolonged, as it is critical that winning organisations focus on the critical few highest value tasks.

Winning organisations that demonstrate this characteristic will have:

- The discipline to plan tasks and act on the few highest value opportunities
- Evidence of using the Pareto principle in prioritising effort
- Resources assigned to tasks as defined in the plan

32. No more than five critical tasks at a time are assigned to a person

Winning organisations are disciplined in focusing on the few high-leverage tasks. This also applies to individuals in the organisation. Limiting critical improvement or discretionary tasks to a maximum of five at any one time maintains focus on the priority tasks.

It is a common trap for capable people in an organisation to be too busy. This means that the person has more tasks to complete than the available time will permit. In this situation, some tasks are not going to get done as they were intended. Unfortunately, it is often the highest value work that does not get done.

Example:

A large manufacturing organisation reviewed the progress of key tasks. The organisation had done a good job of assigning them. One highly capable manager identified that he had 40 key tasks assigned.

When asked how he managed all these tasks, he answered, 'I just focus on the ones I can do and leave the rest.' Most of the tasks were not going to be completed. They could be done the following year, so he reasoned that he would never run out of work.

In this situation, the person assigning work has left it to the discretion of the employee to decide what he/she works on. Another person had 10 key tasks. She said that she had four or five very easy tasks, and provided she did those, she did not care about the difficult ones. But unfortunately, the difficult ones were the high-value ones in this case.

To achieve value focus, critical tasks must be limited to five at any given time. This ensures that each of the tasks are important and that the person assigned is not distracted or spread too thin to be effective. As each task is completed new tasks can be added.

Organisational effectiveness must ensure that work management systems support the value focus planning system by keeping critical tasks within achievable limits.

Winning organisations demonstrating this characteristic will have:

- Effective controls in work management systems to ensure that critical tasks are assigned within limits
- Critical tasks are assigned from the planning and scheduling system

33. Employees have an expectation that they will be held accountable and fairly rewarded for their work.

Winning organisations require motivated employees who seek accountability and believe that they will be fairly rewarded for their work.

The leadership must create a culture where trust, respect, fairness, courage, honesty and care for others is positively demonstrated. This culture is not achieved by highly prescriptive pay differentials, but rather a belief developed over time that what the leadership does and what everyone does together determines how well the organisation performs.

Employees must be confident that they will be rewarded fairly based on their contribution and the organisation's overall performance. People who are invited to contribute their full will and effort need to know:

- What is in it for you?
- What is in it for me?
- What is in it for us together?
- What is in it for everyone else?

Winning organisations are focused on the tasks that create the most value. The belief that one will be rewarded over time based upon the value they create motivates people to do their best. This belief is central to a performance-driven culture.

Fons Trompenaar described two distinctly different beliefs that can be used to explain differing cultures. Trompenaar identified that:

- Universalism cultures -have a high regard for rules applied fairly to people
- Particularism cultures -place a high regard on relationships, so what is fair varies significantly based upon the situation and who is involved

Family businesses that are successful over several generations must balance particularism and universalism well. They must generate value and remain competitive while balancing birthright appointments with the best person for each role.

Non-family member beliefs about their future within family organisations can be particularly crucial. Whether there is an explicit understanding of how people are to be fairly rewarded for their effort or not, there is always an expectation of fairness. If people form the belief that they are not being adequately recognised and rewarded for their contribution, then they will seek to redress the balance.

The role of third parties who try to speak on behalf of certain people as a combined voice can sometimes pose difficulties for employees, leaders and organisations. It is the leadership of the organisation that must be clear on how the core values underpin the culture. The presence of a third party may lead to a sense of outsourcing care and communication. This can create a dependency or lack of accountability. The most important relationship in a winning organisation is between the organisation and its people, where the organisation is represented by the leadership.

Example:

> While being held to account for your work does entail some carrot and stick measures (there must be consequences), in an interdependent culture the prime concern is ensuring that everyone stays safe. As a result, feedback is welcomed and individuals are receptive to opportunities to learn and improve. Standards become owned and improved through an inclusive culture where feedback is frequent and constructively acted upon. No one wants to be injured at work and no one wants somebody working for them to be injured. Everyone wants to work safely. So why do so many people get hurt? Why do third-party organisations so often say that management does not care about safety?
>
> When organisations successfully transition from poor to good safety performance, the all-important change occurs in the culture and the behaviour of leaders. Dupont identified that excellence in safety required the culture of organisations to move from dependent to interdependent (reference DuPont Bradley Curve).
>
> Dependent culture is characterised by people doing what they are instructed to do to comply with safety rules.
>
> Interdependent culture is characterised by people actively demonstrating their 'care value' to proactively look out for each other. In an interdependent culture the workforce is engaged, authorised and held accountable for what they do or do not do. This applies to people in leadership roles as much as anyone else.
>
> In a dependent culture, managers or external authorities legislate the rules. In an interdependent culture, measurement and feedback on safety is sought and valued by all, and all are encouraged to contribute.
>
> Fundamental to achieving this outcome is values-driven leadership, clarity, accountability and the belief that differential reward and recognition (in

terms of not hurting fellow humans) will apply based upon what people do or don't do. This cannot be achieved in situations where people depend exclusively on others to keep them safe.

Winning organisations take effective actions to manage poor performance. Tolerating poor performance decreases motivation and the discretionary contributions of other employees. Leaders who delegate or outsource the responsibility for dealing with chronic poor performance lose track of the fact that the status quo is not acceptable.

The leader must always behave in a positive manner regarding core values and this includes having the courage to follow through with discipline including dismissal if warranted in a timely manner.

The leader should always seek to improve the performance of every team member. Like any plan, if the chosen improvement action is not achieving the required outcomes within the timeframe set then escalation may be required.

Example:

An industrial organisation had developed a problem with many chronic underperforming employees. There had been a string of cases over several years where most people who had been fired by management were subsequently reinstated through external arbitration. In most cases this was due to poor management of work and work performance by leaders.

One leader made it very clear to an employee that if the required performance improvement was not achieved within a certain time that his employment would likely be terminated. The third-party representative told the employee that they would get him reinstated if his role was terminated.

The leader respectfully acknowledged that there was an external arbitration process who may order re-instatement, however, the company would continue to demand the required performance. The leader advised that no one had yet gone to external arbitration twice and been reinstated. In this case, the resolve of the leader was effective in convincing the employee of the need to improve. It was the leader's accountability to escalate actions to achieve the required performance and to do this respectfully within the legislative circumstances that exist. The leader focused on what he could control.

Winning organisations have effective, values-driven leadership that assigns clear tasks and holds people to account fairly for their performance.

Winning organisations demonstrating this characteristic will have:

- Clear policy regarding the reward and recognition of employees
- Employees who believe they are paid fairly for their performance
- Critical tasks or projects provided in writing and accepted by the person accountable
- Regular feedback on the progress of critical tasks
- Leadership that is trusted to be fair (positively demonstrates core values)
- Leaders who take effective action to address poor performance

34. Individual performance assessment is always aligned to the overall performance of the team

Winning organisations assess individual performance as part of fairness in rewarding performance. Tasks assigned to employees are set from the planning system that is the approved best pathway for the organisation to achieve the goals required.

Individual performance must be considered a subset to team performance. This means that an individual could be rewarded differentially to the overall team, although overall team performance must be consistent with overall business performance.

The purpose of a performance system is to improve the performance of the organisation by improving the capability of employees. Too often these systems lose this purpose and instead become obsessed with generating a rating. This can become a demotivating exercise for both the leader and the individual.

Obviously, some people will perform better than others at any given time. The purpose is always to improve. This applies whether the person is performing to an excellent level or is performing poorly. There may be people who are unable to meet the requirements of the role and need to be disciplined or even fired, but this is not the purpose of the performance system.

Another common problem occurs if tasks are not derived from the organisation's plan. In this situation, there can be a divergence of individual performance ratings from the organisation's overall performance. It can be dangerous if the tasking of individuals is not directly linked to organisational performance, as many individuals can receive high-performance ratings even when the organisation is performing poorly. Effective performance systems must ensure that goals and objectives for individuals are derived from the value-focused plan for the organisation.

People need to understand how their work links to the bottom line performance of their team and the organisation. The stronger the linkage the more likely that aligning individual and team rewards will be viewed as fair and reasonable. In this regard, the design of reward processes need to balance individual, immediate team and wider organisation factors to achieve valid and fair recognition and reward.

People need to understand how they are performing.

When key tasks are well-defined and aligned to key output measures, the individual and leader will likely be aligned on the level of performance achieved. When this is the case, the focus can move quickly to defining opportunities for improvement and exploring how to achieve them. When the individual and the leader understand that the purpose of a review is to seek improvement, performance reviews become a less threatening experience and more of a collaboration.

It is important to explore how the leader's behaviour is influencing the performance of the team member. The simple acknowledgement that the leader's behaviour can influence the individual's performance helps balance the openness in communications in performance reviews. Acknowledging the role of the leader in no way confuses accountability for performance; it complements the process of exploring opportunities to improve.

Regular reviewing of performance is essential in building the alignment, engagement and acceptance of objective feedback. When frequent reviews are done, the reviews often take less time to complete. As reviews becomes a more regular experience there will be more straight talk (direct, honest and open).

There should be no surprises if tasks are well-defined and accepted and if there is an agreement on how performance will be measured.

The frequency of reviews will vary depending on the role, the person and the maturity of the relationship. In most cases formal reviews should be scheduled every six to eight weeks. Effective performance management takes time and effort that must be provided for in the standard work routines if it is to be completed effectively.

Despite best intentions, it is not possible to set equally challenging tasks for all employees all the time. Attempting to design a performance system that seeks to rank all employees across a 1–100 scale is likely to be counterproductive. For example, it is possible that a well-performing employee of many years may have one year where the results were below expectations for several good reasons that are acknowledged by the leader. Sometimes factors outside of the employee's control may have impacted the results. Performance systems need discretion built into them to avoid the situation where the system generates an outcome that is not supported by the leader who assigned tasks and is accountable for the performance.

In any performance assessment system, it is critical that the performance of a person at any one time never becomes confused with the individual's self-worth. All people must be treated equally regarding the core values. Deal with the performance only.

Performance systems must be designed to achieve a positive rating on the values continua. Employee performance system design must be aligned with overall organisational performance. Any ratings system must be based upon assessments made by the leader who assigned the work and must allow for a degree of discretionary judgement to ensure fairness. Performance systems are never perfect and hence must have sufficient controls and balances incorporated into the design to be accepted as being fair over the longer -term.

It is important that all employees receive meaningful work that they accept accountability for in conjunction with the right leadership support (including feedback) to be part of a competitive and continuously improving team.

Performance matters and while the consequences of a lower than expected performance may need more urgent corrective action than an outstanding performance, the individual and the leader are always looking for improvement.

It is only possible for the person assigning the work to assess the performance fairly. In designing a performance review system, it is important to make it clear that the final assessment is the decision of the leader who has assigned the tasks and who has been conducting the progress reviews. While there may need to be across organisation controls to ensure relative fairness, these reviews must not be allowed to compromise the role of the leader.

Performance systems do not need to be complicated. A good system only needs to clearly answer the right questions.

Employee:	Role:	Date
Leader:	Role:	Performance Discussion

Rating:	Below Expected ----- As Expected ----- Above Expectations
Why has the rating been justified?	
What could be improved?:	
What could the leader do to help improve?	
What if any developmental initiatives are to be taken?	
Are there any scope of work changes required?	

Figure 15: Example of a simple performance review template

Balancing Stretch vs Achievable in Setting Goals and Tasks

'No pain no gain', 'you never get more than you ask for', 'people need to be driven' and 'only the best will do' are all thoughts that reflect beliefs about how to get more out of people.

It's good to motivate people, to provide confidence in what they can achieve and to provide insights on how to leverage strengths and mitigate weaknesses. When assigning tasks, clarity is the most important factor. As more demanding or complex tasks are assigned, it is important to recognise that the probability of success may become less certain.

Stretch targets have more uncertainty as to the outcome and you need to account for this in planning and task assignment.

If a research project is undertaken that disproves a theory and the project was conducted to an excellent standard, then the person accountable should be rewarded for how well the research was conducted and not the fact that the theory was disproved. Often stretch goals or objectives require the person to consider different ideas and pathways from those that would normally be the case with incremental goals.

Expect to assign some stretch goals in the highest leverage areas. It is always important to consider the capability of the person when assigning tasks and this is particularly true for stretch tasks.

It is doing the right work that advances the organisation.

It is essential that the leader and the person assigned the task have adequately covered the range of possible outcomes. Alignment around the risk of achieving certain outcomes is an important quality aspect from planning that should be understood in task assignment.

You may prefer to assign stretch goals as a portion of the work in high-leverage areas, provided that the risks of certain outcomes are clearly understood and agreed upon by the leader and the person accountable for executing the task.

Example:

In a greenfield organisation, the production manager is assigned a task to commit at least 15% of rostered time to safety work; with a view that this will significantly contribute to eliminating medical treatment injuries from occurring within the workplace. Given that the organisation was new, it was unclear what level of safety performance would be achieved with this 15% commitment of time.

Both the leader and the task owner in this case were guided by a belief that if the right amount of effort was applied and the theory was correct, then the desired safety outcome should be achieved. In this case, frequently reviewing the safety time commitment and the resultant safety results achieved was the critical measure for task execution.

Managing and understanding risk is a critical aspect of successful leadership. Winning organisations recognise that all risk cannot be eliminated as this would result slow decision making and low rate of improvement. A proportion of resources within an operationally excellent organisation should be devoted to high-risk/high-gain tasks. In these circumstances effective controls are applied to mitigate the impact of the higher risk.

Winning organisations demonstrating this characteristic will have:
- Performance systems that differentially reward individual performance and align with overall organisational performance
- A focus on the improvement of performance systems

35. The level of effectiveness in finding the right person for the right role at the right time is measured

Winning organisations use data to guide decision-making.

This applies to organisational effectiveness in ensuring that the right person is available at the right time, in the right role, doing the right work in the right way.

To build an organisation that has the right people capabilities to reliably perform the work requires a talent management planning process. The inputs to this planning process must include:

- Feedback from employees on how well their expectations of leaders have been met
- How well they have been engaged by their leader
- How well they are completing key tasks assigned
- Overall performance level
- What improvement actions have been decided
- What other roles they could do
- If a role change is recommended and if so, in what time frame?
- If there is at least one readily available successor for the role
- Objective measures (productivity, absence data, turnover, exit interview feedback, cost of talent management, replacement timeframes, percentage of roles with the right people in the right role)

A succession plan is expected that estimates the likely timeframes of incumbents in roles and assigns trackable actions that will ensure that the organisation can seamlessly fill critical roles that become vacant.

Example:

A lean flat organisation involved in manufacturing was contemplating its first attempt at succession planning. On first review, the same person was identified as a potential successor for four more senior roles. This identified a potential problem, more potential successors were required to avoid the possibility of not having people ready for all four senior roles. The senior management also realised that they did not know what the current role incumbents' career plans were. It was decided that some estimate from people in key roles of their likely time in the role was needed.

The other important consideration was how long it would take to train a suitable person to be fully competent in each critical role. More than six

months was required to recruit and train people for the critical roles due to high technical knowledge component.

With the estimates of tenure and discipline for a successor to be only allocated once a plan was completed. Discussions with successors regarding their future were welcomed. By better alignment of capability and aspiration, a forward-looking plan was developed that ensured minimal gaps in the key roles. This supported investment in training and recruitment strategies to mitigate the risk of not having people ready for key roles when anticipated.

36. Employee turnover is stable and at a rate less than 10% per year

Winning organisations require an efficient and focused execution of work. Some employee turnover is healthy. However, if turnover exceeds 10% per year, it becomes a burden on stability and suggests incompatibilities between employee aspirations and the organisation.

This level of turnover is usually due to expectations not being met by the organisation or the individual, or both. You need to understand the value proposition of the organisation and the role, and match this with the person selected.

A common mistake is to hire someone of a higher capability than required. This results in frustrated employees who will seek to change their situation. Poor leadership is another common cause of good people leaving. Remuneration must be competitive. However, even when a person says they are leaving for higher pay, it is often only one contributing factor. Feeling valued, successful and sufficiently challenged are motivators for employees to remain.

Example:

An industrial manufacturing company decided they could improve performance by implementing a Six Sigma program. The leadership decided to implement belt training across the organisation.

Many of the roles had long timeframes before incumbents became competent in their roles. Some roles required over four years of in-house experience and training before being considered competent. The organisation had turnover of around 12% per year.

Flexibility in the organisation was hampered by a high number of people requiring training. Delays in hiring replacements for leaving employees also meant that teams were short staffed; which further contributed to difficulties in meeting the training schedule, work not being done to standard and frustration from experienced employees trying to do multiple jobs.

The ability to attract new people was made more difficult due to the poor reputation of the organisation. The Six-Sigma training was just another complication. Six Sigma training sessions were poorly attended because people could not be freed up to attend. The Six Sigma training was highly sought after by those employees with a motivation to find a job elsewhere.

This organisation needed to analyse and improve how they hired and managed people before attempting any Six Sigma training. The priority was to speed up the hiring process to ensure that there were enough employees to get the work done. Recognition of the number of hours of training meant that the number of employees needed to be increased above target levels.

37. All employees are engaged in seeking to minimise variation, including how work is planned and executed

Winning organisations seek to engage all their employees in improvement and in reducing variation. This must include how work is planned and executed. It is often the variation in how work is executed that causes variation in how processes perform.

Winning organisations develop a culture that is shared by all employees that appreciates each person's role in minimising variation. Training on the effect of variation is usually provided in the "way we work" program provided for employees.

Engagement Surveys and Their Place

It has become relatively common, and perhaps even trendy, to conduct employee engagement surveys in large organisations. Many of the organisations conducting surveys, however, are failing to provide adequate feedback or take effective action to improve engagement. Employees can become frustrated and cynical in their views of leaders who conduct surveys where no action follows.

A common problem is that if leaders do not clearly understand what their roles are and do not understand the benefits of engaging their people, then the data from engagement surveys is not acted upon.

Keep in mind that many, if not all the leaders may never have experienced working in an engaged workplace themselves. So, it should not be taken for granted that the leadership understands what needs to be done or what benefits would be derived from improved engagement of employees.

Example:

A large organisation involved in providing essential health services to the community had identified a need to improve leadership's capability to engage the workforce.

The organisation had conducted a survey annually over many years. The chief executive hoped that the latest survey would show encouraging improvements over the previous results. She wanted to see improvement over previous years as a confirmation that her actions taken during the year were working.

She sent emails and provided video messages to employees asking them to complete the survey. In the end, less than 40% of employees took the time to fill it out the survey. The response from those who did reply reflected a low degree of engagement.

The result was predictable; the middle to lower-level managers described the survey as a waste of time and felt it had nothing to do with them. Middle managers were one of the lowest survey respondent groups.

Of course, engagement had everything to do with the managers.

The CEO had failed to first engage and align the leadership on what was required and why. If the leader would not complete the survey positively, then why would they expect anything better from the employees?

Employees who are asked to complete surveys and then get no feedback or see no change as a result will judge their leadership negatively.

Figure 16: Key actionable data that may be useful from an engagement survey

1. I know how my work contributes to the success of the company

2. I strive to do my very best to help the company be successful

3. I have the tools (technology/equipment) needed do my job well

4. I have the skills, training and development needed to do my job

5. I am motivated to do my best at my job

6. I feel valued and recognized for the work I do

7. I get a sense of accomplishment from my work

8. I have the authority to make decisions consistent with my level of work

9. My job makes full use of my knowledge and abilities

10. I clearly understand my job and what is expected of me

11. I have a healthy and safe work environment

12. I feel comfortable raising safety concerns in the workplace to my supervisor / manager/ the person I report to

13. Within my team, employees are respected

14. In my team, we are all trying to improve our performance

15. At my site, we have the people we need to get the job done

16. Gives me constructive feedback on my work

17. Makes sure our team celebrates our success

18. Respects me

19. Cares about my well-being

20. Makes a genuine effort to help me improve my performance

21. Is not afraid to deal with issues

22. Is competent

23. Is honest and trustworthy

24. Takes time to let me know my efforts are appreciated

25. Effectively deals with poor performance on our team

26. I am proud to tell people I work for

27. I would, without hesitation, highly recommend xxx to a friend seeking

28. Given the opportunity I tell others great things about working here

Executing

People are required to define and complete tasks. Only in the execution of a task is there the potential to create value. 'How well is the organisation able to execute tasks according to plan?' is an important question to answer.

When a project plan is clearly defined, the execution phase is about following the plan as closely as possible. Divergence from the plan can only result in lost value in the form of scope creep (extra work not planned for) or delayed completion dates, all of which add extra costs. Errors, slippages in time, distraction from critical path jobs, scope creep, damage and environmental factors are always likely to impact a project to some degree. It's fundamental to execute the work as close as possible to the plan to achieve best results.

Before moving a project into execution, the organisation must be ready. Making sure that a clearly defined scope and the resources to complete the project within the boundary limits chosen is critical to success.

Even the risk of having to change key people during the execution phase should be considered. Changing the project manager once things have started usually results in some delays/ scope changes and poorer project outcomes. Getting things right the first time is the goal.

Nothing happens until somebody does something; no value is created until the idea turns into reality. It is in the execution phase where the rubber hits the road and value is created or destroyed.

Many great ideas fail due to poor execution. However, no matter how good the execution phase is, if the business case was flawed from the outset the result will still be a poor return on investment.

It is essential that the definition, design and planning has been completed before moving into the execution phase. The execution phase is where the major investment occurs. Once the decision has been made to commit to a project or task it is essential that the leadership are focused on getting the right work done on time and in the right way.

Execution defines what must be done by whom, with what, when and in what way. Value is created by transforming inputs into the outputs within the time, resource, risk and ethical limits described in the plan.

38. The organisational design clearly describes how authority and resources are organised to achieve the vision

Winning organisations are designed to achieve the vision. All employees must be able to describe how the organisational design distributes authority and supports this vision.

The purpose of an organisational structure is to distribute authority and resources to effectively deliver the business objectives.

Once an organisation has a clear vision and has determined the goals and objectives, the leadership must consider the work that needs to be done and how it will be organised. How an organisation is designed reflects the mindset of the leadership. The organisational structure will impose controls and limits that impact flexibility, information flow and will define where power resides.

The organisational design will have a significant influence on the culture of the organisation and will influence how people behave. Imagine an organisation that hires in the brightest new talent with an aim to inject a dynamic, flexible and innovative capability, then places these people in roles where they're reporting to people who are used to controlling decision-making and have a vested interest in maintaining the status quo. In this scenario, there may be an initial flurry of activity before the new talent either learns to conform, leaves the organisation, or successfully mounts a coup to usurp the established system.

How the organisation is designed has a big influence on how the organisation will operate. The design must support the way the organisation wants to operate. Flat hierarchy for example, supports faster decision making and more delegated authority.

The distribution of authority has a large impact on how the organisation will function. Many organisations are designed from the top down and in this approach, power is progressively distributed from the senior executive down. While this makes logical sense given that the person doing the design is the senior executive, it can result in the creation of more layers of management than are really needed. Additional layers slow down decision-making and may not benefit the efficient operation of the frontline processes (which is where value is created).

Another way to look at the organisational design is to focus on the key processes first and then define the key operational roles or floor level roles required, and only then add the management or leadership roles.

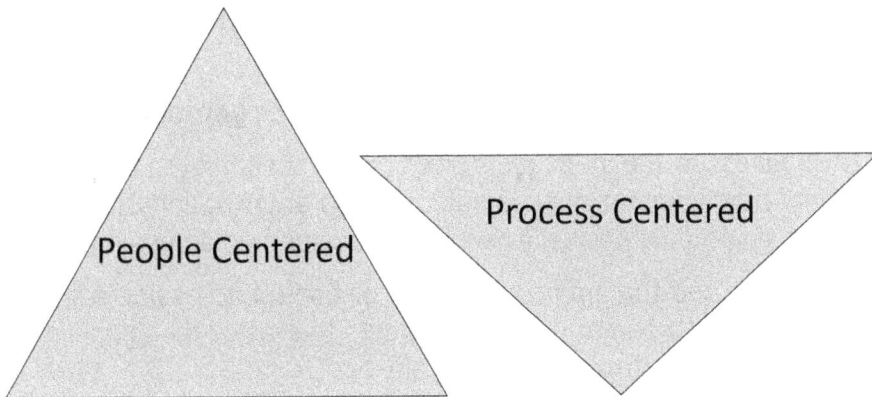

Figure 17: Top-down vs process first approach to organisational design

A bottom-up driven viewpoint in design keeps the focus on what the value driving processes need. The 'process first approach' to organisational design can also be a powerful symbol that demonstrates that the leadership respects and understands where value is created and understands that the purpose of the organisation is to support the efficient operation of these processes.

The design of an organisation is best created using clear principles or theories that can be consistently applied. This will support role clarity, consistency, efficiency and change management over time.

Elliot Jacques (*Requisite Organisation*, published 1997) provided useful theories around organisational design that can support building a winning organisation. *Requisite Organisation* is recommended reading before designing any organisation. It provides clear models and theories that are useful in deciding the purpose of roles and how a role relates to other roles.

From the perspective of a winning organisation, a key purpose of leadership roles is to improve the ability of the team to achieve its goals. It is essential to clearly define the purpose of every role.

The term 'manager' is often used to describe 'the person in control' or 'the person in charge'—the 'boss'. Make no mistake, the value created from the work of the manager comes from the impact that manager has on how the team operates. Managers who have tasking authority, must be effective leaders. They are measured over time by how well the team performs.

In a winning organisation, performance must continuously improve over time at a rate greater than the competition.

How Many Levels of Management Does an Organisation Require?

In small businesses, the manager is often the owner and even the operator, so one level of management may be sufficient. As organisations become larger and more complex, work usually needs to be distributed across multiple roles.

Jacques introduced the notion of a 'span of control' to assist in the design of an organisation. Span of control considers the tasks, the capability of the person and the standard work of each role.

Starting at the process leadership level first, the following key questions need to be considered in designing the organisation:

- How many people could that person lead?
  - o How diverse is the technical skill set of the people reporting to that leader?
  - o How complex is the work?
- How does this process and the team that supports it relate to other processes and their teams (customers/suppliers)?

The leadership must be able to improve the performance of the processes. This is achieved by influencing the people who directly undertake the tasks required to operate the processes. The leadership must: assign clear tasks, provide the training needed, review progress, listen, observe, develop the people and learn how the processes are functioning.

The leader must understand the work of the team. However, it is a mistake to assume that the most technically capable person will be the most effective leader. The most significant component of the leader's role requires:

- Decision-making
- Influencing people
- Problem solving
- Planning
- Assigning clear tasks
- Providing effective routines and systems
- Utilising the capability of the team
- Developing capability
- Tracking work execution progress to ensure that the organisation is on track to achieve its goals

Typically, a leader can only effectively support up to fifteen team members where they are doing substantially the same work. If the work of team members is not very similar, the maximum number of direct reports drops to nine.

When a leader has too many direct reports it is generally the longer-term work such as coaching and development of people that is dropped. Effective leadership requires significant time demands from a leader who fully engages with each team member.

For all roles, it is essential to establish standard work routines that will help provide a common understanding around how, when and what to communicate. Standard work routines represent the daily, weekly, monthly and annual meetings, planning tasks, process review tasks, key communications and routine tasks that are best completed at set dates and times. Completing the standard work routines will confirm more precisely how many direct reports a leader can support.

The span of the control model is helpful in determining when and why an additional management level is required. It is important in the organisational design to clearly define where the boundaries and overlaps are between levels of leadership.

It is never productive to have two leaders accountable for the same work. This will guarantee confusion and reduced ownership. Sometimes managers see their role as reviewing the work of their team members. Review is not justification for a role; all roles must have legitimate value adding work to contribute.

Many organisations seek to concentrate authority in higher levels of the organisation with a view to achieving better control of expenditure. Costs are, however, an outcome of actions taken by people. Any inability to assign the resources needed to complete the standard work in a timely manner will inevitably contribute to delays and waste. Employees who feel that they do not have sufficient resources or authorities to do the work of their role will feel untrusted and their ownership will be diminished. This eventually becomes a barrier to accessing that person's full capability as they wait to be directed from above, even though they know what needs to be done.

Winning organisations establish effective feedback measures and controls that allow everyone the appropriate authorities and accountabilities to do their standard work.

Example:

Process operators in a smelter were required to gather process samples for analysis. Results were then sent to the plant manager to review and decide on any process setpoint changes.

The process operators received no feedback regarding the samples they took. The plant manager reviewed the sample analyses each morning. The process operated 24/7. Why wouldn't the results from the samples be provided to the process operator who could then adjust process set points within defined limits without delay?

The answer was, 'because they were not the qualified'. The analyses did not seem to match what was supposed to happen from a theory perspective. Upon review, it was found that the process operators placed little importance on the quality of the samples taken, and in some cases, operators were taking all the samples for their shift in the first hour, rather than at regular intervals during their shift.

The first thought could be that the process operators couldn't be trusted. However, once the plant manager thought about this some more, he made the decision to provide the training, the systems and the control response guidelines to the process operators to act on.

The operators were then taking the samples with the purpose of getting feedback that they needed to make process control decisions as part of their role. This made them feel more trusted and important, and created a 24/7 response capability that greatly improved process stability. The process operators' self-esteem increased, and they became more interested in learning and taking on more process control decision-making. The plant manager was then able to focus time on other areas of improvement.

The key point is that winning organisations establish the systems, training, communication and authorities with a view to supporting decision-making and ownership of processes as close to real-time as possible, and that means as close to the floor as possible.

There is no greater example of how powerful this is, than at Toyota where the assembly line operator has the authority to stop the entire production line if the process moves outside of defined limits. If the production line is down, management goes to the process to work with their team to understand and solve the root cause of the problem.

Organisational Silos

Organisations can develop vertical silos that may become barriers in creating a winning organisation. These can be minimised by clearly defining horizontal role relationships and by ensuring that all roles are properly designed and connected to the fundamental business processes.

In designing an organisation, the objective is to deliver the required work with the minimum number of levels necessary. The design objective is to minimise duplication or sub-utilisation of resources.

The concept of 'do it once and do it right' is a sound principle that should guide how and where to place the service or support functions. Always test whether a role added has a discrete set of accountabilities that do not overlap with another role. For example, if a role is accountable for service delivery then that role should have authority over the service delivery processes, including the budget and team leadership for the service.

It is never productive to confuse or overlap role accountabilities. Imagine a car driving along with a left-hand side driver and a right-hand side driver. A tree appears in the distance. The left-hand driver pulls left to avoid the tree and the right-hand driver pulls right; the car drives into the tree.

Next time in the same situation, the left-hand driver assumes that the right-hand driver will turn right, the right-hand driver assumes that if he did not turn to avoid the tree the left-hand driver would turn left as he did before; the car still hits the tree. It is always better to have one driver with the clear authority to act so that the driver can make decisions in a timely manner.

There are always limits to discretion; using our car scenario, these limits include road rules, traffic lights, car maintenance and signs that are designed to keep discretion within safe limits.

Sometimes alliances with other organisations to achieve the best service and technical support can simplify the organisational design and help maintain the focus on what is important. In many cases, there is not sufficient demand or development opportunities for an in-house resource. Outsourcing to an organisation where the demand is higher may give better results.

Deciding which core competencies to retain in the organisation and which services to outsource can help with efficiency and simplification. Some common examples of services that are often outsourced include IT, financial auditing, emergency services, recruitment, transportation, training, administrative support and maintenance. Winning organisations recognise what is core work and seek advantages from outsourcing the work where it is efficient to do so.

Wherever silos exist in the organisational structure, it is essential to recognise that there is an elevated risk of across silo breakdowns in communication and planning. An emphasis on transparency and shared feedback metrics from the processes that transcend the silos is critical to avoiding waste.

Managers can mitigate risk across organisational silos by:

- Ensuring that the process feedback measures are common and transparent to each area
- Ensuring that planning and communication requires collaborative input across the organisational silo
- Establishing work routines where representation across the silos share information on a regular basis

To Centralise or Decentralise Decision-making?

There does not appear to be a clear answer concerning the question of whether decentralisation is better than centralisation when it comes to organisational design. Often organisations lean one way only to lean back the other if the perceived balance is skewed too much either way.

One example of this that occurs quite frequently in resource companies involves maintenance. Maintenance requires a close relationship with production. As a result, the decentralise argument is based upon the better alignment of maintenance with production needs, hence placing maintenance resources alongside production teams.

The counter-argument is that maintenance needs to be a separate department led by specialists to ensure that the work is being done competently. It is common for managers to perceive a benefit when they switch from the current preference to the alternative. Changing reporting structures creates a leadership focal point (Hawthorne Effect). Therefore, anyone who has been around long enough, will probably experience shifts between centralisation and decentralisation.

In the maintenance example, it follows that effective planning that incorporates maintenance and production work is the critical activity that will deliver sustainable benefits beyond centralisation or decentralisation biases.

Winning organisations will understand that duplication is wasteful. In all organisational design options, achieving local understanding and ownership of roles, systems and processes is the essential determinant of success.

People in the organisation need to understand the theories used that led to the organisational structure chosen.

Example:

In a manufacturing organisation, the senior executive team was aligned around the organisation being designed as a matrix. Matrix was interpreted as accountability being shared across a team of executives.

The problem was that none of the senior executives could explain clearly what a matrix organisation was and how it operated. The term 'matrix' suggested a complex set of interrelationships, where functions were tasked horizontally as well as vertically and people could have multiple managers assigning work.

Managers were confused as to how the organisation was intended to work. One manager expressed the view, 'I cannot trust getting the required work done unless I control it myself.'

Without a clear understanding of how the organisational design was supposed to work and without integrated planning or clear role accountabilities the confusion was not surprising. A great deal of waste occurred due to the lack of clarity; managers were making decisions based upon their individual viewpoints which, in turn, created more confusion and waste.

Confusion concerning the organisational design theory or intent can create a high degree of duplication and rework, leading to accountability gaps and waste.

A detailed description of how roles fit and work together that is supported by common planning and common shared performance measures is required.

The balance between centralisation and de-centralisation should be driven by how best to achieve standardisation and ownership. Everyone has heard the 'we are from corporate and we are here to help' phrase. This reflects the frequent organisational separation that can occur between head office and distributed sites. Policies, systems and initiatives designed from the corporate centre which are then rolled out to the masses often result in lower local acceptance and compliance than initiatives designed locally.

The Importance of Ownership and Acceptance in Deciding on Organisational Design

Results = quality x acceptance (reference: *The Six Sigma Leader* by Peter Pande).

If either the quality or the acceptance is low, then the result will also be low (or even zero). Delivering results requires a quality solution that is understood, accepted and supported by the people involved.

If people do not understand why changes are being made, then it is difficult for them to provide support. If people feel that they are doing something for someone else's benefit and cannot translate how it benefits them or the organisation, it is unlikely they will fully support it.

Values-based leadership understands the need to communicate and exchange information between people in a respectful and trustworthy way. A powerful and commonly used approach in safety management to help understand what happened in an incident, is to simply ask 'why' five times. 'Five Why' questioning provides a deeper understanding of cause and effect relationships and serves as a simple method for gaining confidence and acceptance in choosing a certain direction.

Communication requires time and that time investment is essential if acceptance of a change is going to be high. Remember, communication is two-way and for any change to be supported there must be effective communication.

Many organisations have found success in adopting small central departments that develop common systems, methods and standards using authorised and connected local champions. This is sometimes referred to as the 'Hybrid Organisational Model'.

The Hybrid Organisational Model is an alternative to the Centralise/Decentralise Model where the importance of local acceptance in change is recognised. The hybrid model is specifically designed to achieve the best balance between quality and acceptance and has the benefit of requiring only a small central support resource. By effectively coordinating the contributions from local champions, a high degree of local ownership can be achieved for enterprise-wide decisions. Part of the local champion's role is to contribute to corporate-wide initiatives.

Example:

A global resource company had evolved over many decades using a decentralised model. Each location had developed their own safety systems over many years. The local safety standards and language were different.

The organisation had evolved through acquisition. As part of the latest acquisition, savings were sought in corporate overheads. The new senior leadership was accustomed to a highly-centralised approach to decision-making and was seeking a move in this direction, but without growing the cost of the corporate office.

Each site had many conceptually similar safety systems. However, the language and supporting materials were different. They all had a high degree of ownership and attachment to their systems. To replace all the systems with one new system would be expensive so it was decided to adopt the hybrid model. Corporate would be accountable for defining the standards for the entire organisation and each location would be accountable for determining how they would comply.

Corporate utilised the network of local champions to develop new systems and materials for the entire organisation. The approach was chosen to avoid duplication, non-value adding cost and ensure high local acceptance.

This hybrid model proved to be very effective. Common standards could be developed quickly and at low cost by using the champion network. Allowing suitable discretion at a local level was perceived as respectful, trusting and fair. The difficult areas for changes were always those where people had already vested a great deal of effort and emotional capital in a local solution that they believed was working. The hybrid model proved to be a highly cost-effective organisational structure in this case.

Winning organisations that demonstrate this characteristic will have:

- A clearly defined vision and strategy understood by all employees
- A clear theory as to how the organisational design supports the vision
- Roles that are defined and have the appropriate authorities to enable incumbents to work to their capability

39. Levels of management do not exceed six, with a clear theory explaining the value of the work being done at each level

Winning organisations require fast, flexible communications and decision-making. Employees must have the required authority to act. Each managerial level has clear and unique scope. The maximum number of management levels is six. The more levels, the greater the complexity and the greater the potential for waste and confusion.

Levels of Work Model (interpreted from Elliot Jacques work):

- **Level 1** roles (frontline leaders) typically focus on work that needs to be completed today and this week. Frontline roles typically deal with short-term feedback tasks. At least 80% of the role will be focused on today and the week ahead.
- **Level 2** roles would be expected to spend around 80% of the effort on tasks that will have an outcome a week to a month into the future. The planning horizon for this level is one to three months out. Just because the focus is longer term does not mean that the role is not involved in daily interaction with people and processes.
- **Level 3** roles are expected to devote 80% of the effort on tasks having an impact over a period of months to years usually with the accountability for building three-year plans. Once again, level 3 must be involved in daily standard work with people and processes.
- **Level 4** roles devote 80% of the effort to one to three years in the future with accountability for five-year plans being common. Once again, level 4 must be involved in daily standard work with people, systems and processes.
- **Level 5** roles devote 80% of time in the three to ten-year timeframe. This work may include expanding networks or new lines and building relationships and the reputation of the organisation with external stakeholders.
- **Level 6** devotes 80% of time to 10 to 20 years in the future. Level 5 and Level 6 roles still have regular interaction with people and processes. Level 5 and Level 6 spend a significant effort in creating new thinking and new opportunities for creating value. The pressure on a new Level 6 CEO is such that 20-year horizon decisions may need to be

made within only a few months to years of being in the role. While the consequence of the decision may not be clear for many years in terms of real value created, the thinking at the time must extend 20 years out in many cases. The ambiguity and risk in terms of value are much higher at level 6 than at level 3.

If the level 6 role incumbent is focused on work at level 3, the organisation is at serious long-term risk. When more senior roles attempt to become involved in the work of more junior roles, authority and accountability will become confused and distrust will grow. Perhaps even more problematic is when senior leaders fall into the trap of micromanaging they are not focused on doing the work that only the senior manager could and should be doing.

Organisations rarely need more than six levels, yet some organisations create many more.

Having more levels than required can be legitimate for a defined period, due to succession planning needs. Additional managerial levels are sometimes motivated by senior leaders who are distancing themselves from accountability.

More levels of management than required adds complexity and cost and will slow down decision-making, reduce ownership of work, and erode the acceptance of accountability and transparency within the organisation.

It is essential that the leadership be considered as one chain. The longer the chain (more levels of management) the more capacity for variation and misalignment. For a chain to be able to function all the links must be intact. The strength of any chain is determined by the weakest link.

An important part of the standard work of all leaders is to go to where the value-adding work takes place and test for alignment.

Example:

In a commodity-based organisation, the CEO was concerned about slim profit margins. He called for costs to be cut where possible and he specifically directed that overtime levels be cut.

At this time, however, the frontline supervisors were desperately preoccupied with getting enough overtime resources to meet safety crew limits to scrape through to the next shift. They were spending on average an hour a shift calling people on the overtime list, almost begging them to come into work. In this situation, the leadership feedback processes had broken down.

The CEO's message and needs were completely incongruent to what the frontline supervisors were experiencing and thinking. They needed their managers' assistance. If the senior managers had spent more time in the workplace, seeking to understand what the issues were at the floor level, then alignment would have occurred quickly.

This is a critical aspect of 'Lean Thinking'. Management needs to spend time where the work takes place, so they can observe, listen and build a common understanding of the critical issues.

When the leadership can communicate up and down the chain effectively and there is alignment around a clear plan of action, results can be achieved that previously might have been considered impossible. When all levels of an organisation have a common understanding of the critical issues, it is more likely that they will be able to respond.

In winning organisations, a maximum of six levels is sufficient. Adding more layers and more departments increases the complexity of communication and alignment and slows down the response times on critical issues. From time to time, it may be necessary to add roles to support succession planning and people development provided that the changes have a clear purpose and a definite timeframe.

Winning organisations that demonstrate this characteristic will have:
- No more than six levels of management
- A clear theory as to the purpose of each level of management and how each role fits into the overall leadership chain

40. The number of direct reports fits within effective limits

Winning organisations understand the people-related work of effective managers. Organisational design ensures that the number of reporting roles does not exceed effective limits. Effective reporting limits are typically less than nine when there are diverse role mixes, or less than fifteen if there are common or similar role mixes.

In small teams of people:

- The level of interaction and opportunity for communication is high
- It is much easier for the leader to coach and see what is going on
- The team can function without as much structure and organisation
- The leader is much closer to the process

As team size becomes larger, the leader must have more structure and organisation as there is less time available to engage with each individual team member. Consider what a reasonable level of time per week would be. Assume that 30 minutes per week may be sufficient. That means the leader would need to find four and a half hours per week for individual engagement with a nine-person team.

Effective leaders need to understand the scope of work that they are accountable for. This does not mean that they need to be an expert in every role within their team.

The leaders need to know how the outputs of the work connect with the process to create value. This is also important in considering how large a direct reporting team should be. Diverse and highly specialised technical expertise requirements may require smaller teams and more leaders.

In organisations with only three levels of management it is possible to create an organisation larger than a thousand people with the direct reporting limits suggested.

Winning organisations that demonstrate this characteristic will have:

- The number of direct reports to a leader within effective limits of fifteen for like roles and nine for varied roles

41. All employees are given the authority and resources required to efficiently complete their standard work

Winning organisations require employees to work to their full capability. Fast decision-making is required and to support this all employees need to have the accountability and authority to make decisions relating to the standard work of their role. Effective leadership sets the required controls to achieve this.

Authority can be defined as having the power to assign tasks and consume resources within the accepted standards of the organisation or community. Authority always has boundary conditions or constraints. For example, spending money up to a limit or assigning tasks to specific roles within the standards of the organisation.

Accountability is the ability to be differentially rewarded for the outcome of work. For differential reward to be fair, there must be clear measurable outcomes agreed to by a person who has the required skills and resources (including authorities) to complete the task as specified. If the leader attempts to assign accountability without providing the required authorities, there will, with certainty, be a problem in completing the task as envisioned. People need to know clearly what it is that is required of them and must have the skills and resources required to successfully execute the work assigned.

The roles and responsibilities in the organisation need to reflect the accountabilities required. Employees must have an expectation that they will be held accountable for their work.

Example:

An organisation that wanted to significantly improve its safety performance made it clear to all employees that they had the authority to refuse any work they believed could result in injury to themselves or others.

By doing this, the organisation had increased the accountability of all employees should they have a safety concern. The delegation of this authority gave them the ability to prevent unsafe work and to be held accountable for how they used this authority in their work.

The difference between a workplace where the supervisor or manager is solely accountable for setting the standard and ensuring compliance and one where all employees are accountable is profound. When delegating authority, it remains essential that the leader ensures that the work assigned is being executed as intended and that work outcomes are tracking as

planned. When the team is empowered, the leader's style usually becomes more involved in coaching and less in directing.

Significant effort is required to establish and maintain clear accountabilities and authorities within an organisation. The time required for this work must be included in the standard work of leaders. Alignment and communication can be assisted by ensuring the entire organisation is connected to the plan and progress tracking metrics.

The use of visual workplace aids and run charts is an excellent time-effective method to quickly learn how a process is performing. Lean 'strategy on a page' uses a poster-style summary of goals and objectives, current performance, future performance required, progress on key tasks and key metrics to communicate progress.

Questions that are common in an organisation that delegates accountability and authority appropriately include:

- Who is accountable?
- What is the priority?
- What resources are available?
- When it will be complete?
- Who else needs to know about this?
- How will we know it is on track?
- How does this task fit in with other tasks?

It's important to map out accountabilities and authorities horizontally and vertically. Key questions that are common are:

- Who is the customer or sponsor?
- Who needs what information?
- Who provides support and in what way is that support invoked?

Just as a winning organisation is a culmination of efforts along a journey, building clear accountability and authority is a constant process of Plan-Do-Check-Act (PDCA) as people constantly seek clarity.

Using the 80/20 rule ensures that the amount of written detail is kept to only what is required to clearly understand who, what, where, when, how and why in the task assignment. The clearer the task assignment and the more focused the critical tasks, the more likely it is that the task will be executed as planned and the faster the review processes will be. It is much better to see milestones being achieved than spend hours reviewing, re-forecasting, re-budgeting and replanning.

Building Winning Organisations

Winning organisations that demonstrate this characteristic will have:

- Employees who take initiative, know their critical tasks and confidently understand their authorities and limits
- Decision-making authority is distributed appropriately so that employees take ownership of their work contribution

42. All roles have defined: the purpose, authorities, accountabilities, skills, relationship to other roles (vertically and horizontally) and performance outputs

Winning organisations require clarity in accountability and authority both vertically and horizontally. Defining horizontal role relationships requires clarity as to how roles relate to processes and reduces organisational silos or gaps.

As the horizontal relationships are described, so too will the customer/ supplier relationships and the measures and flow of information that is required to support process performance. Horizontal relationships are critical to minimising the gaps that can arise from vertical relationships. The organisation must be anchored to value creation and that means all work is assigned from planning and is prioritised using the model to estimate the value across the full end-to-end process.

People—Programming—Technical Model

A model outlined by MacDonald in *Systems Leadership* suggests that all roles include three key components that must be present for that role to be effective. The three components are:

- People—the work of communicating, influencing and training
- Programming/planning—organising, developing routines and standards, allocating time and resources in advance of executing the task
- Technical—physical effort and applying specific knowledge to a task

The model proposes that all roles need all three components and that different roles will have different proportions of those three components. A role with the title of planner would expect to have a high percentage of time in the role dedicated to planning work. A hands-on tradesman operating a lathe would expect to have a high percentage of time allocated to technical work.

What is interesting is how much time in management roles that should be devoted to people work, compared with how much time most managers actually devote to people work. In winning organisations, a vital aspect of the leader's work is improving the performance of the team. As a result, the work of an effective leader must have a dominant people/work component.

Planning must also be a significant component of a leader's work as he/she must support/establish work routines. The technical component of the role should be less than each of the people and the programming components.

However, it is a common error to select managers primarily due to their technical abilities. Understanding the technical aspects of the organisation is undoubtedly valuable, however, managers who gravitate to the technical domain often miss the real opportunity of leading the development of their team's capability. Training people, providing the right information at the right time, delegating down the authority to competent people so that they can own their work and use their full capability is a much more valuable contribution than continuing to be the technical expert.

It is critical that the leader values the people/work component of the role. A leader who has a strong technical background and is not interested in people will never build an engaged team. In some cases, overly technically-focused leaders may even try to make themselves indispensable from a technical knowledge perspective.

A winning organisation requires leaders who value a high component of people and programming work.

Senior leaders must recognise the critical nature of their roles in developing effective work routines and systems that support the organisation down to the floor level. This focuses effort onto the right priorities.

Proportion of work in PPT Model

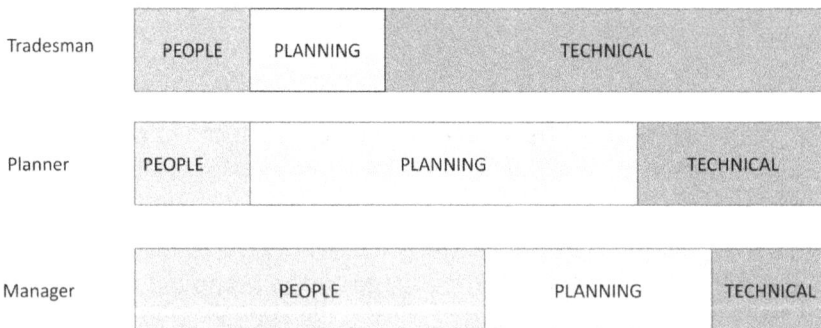

Tradesman	PEOPLE	PLANNING	TECHNICAL
Planner	PEOPLE	PLANNING	TECHNICAL
Manager	PEOPLE	PLANNING	TECHNICAL

Figure 18: Proportion of effort of roles across different types of work using PPT Model

Skills and Training

Training is a continuous effort with the goal of enabling people to achieve the work requirements of their role more effectively.

In many organisations, training effort can seem expensive compared with the visible returns. For training to be valuable it needs to be a transfer of the right knowledge or skills to the individual that is necessary for the person to complete their role.

Competency assessment ensures that both the trainer and the recipient stay focused and expend sufficient effort in confirming mutual understanding. Competency assessment requires a clear articulation of the intended value that will be achieved from the training, which then is the basis for testing. In this way, training effort can be focused more effectively and will provide a better return on investment.

The other important requirement is that the outcomes of the training will be applied in the work environment within a reasonable time. If a person takes too long to apply the learning it is likely the resident skill or 'know-how' will decay. The organisation needs to have competency-based training that is directly utilised in the workplace. The organisation must understand that training is an essential investment derived from planning to support achieving the work outcomes required from the goals and objectives.

The leadership needs to ensure that value is derived from training. While organisations can successfully outsource training delivery, the connection of training outcomes to value in the workplace must be made by the leadership.

All training needs to have a clear purpose that directly links to the standard work that the person will be undertaking. By clearly stating the purpose it makes it much easier to determine what competencies are needed.

All training must include a reinforcement aspect in the workplace.

Even if the training is required and the program is well designed it is important to assess the quality of how the training is delivered. Participant feedback reviews should be conducted.

Maintaining the currency of training content and the connections to the workplace requires the ongoing involvement of influential people including appointed leaders from the workplace. Leader involvement ensures the necessary currency and commitment to the training is not only maintained but is improved over time.

Winning organisations that demonstrate this characteristic will have:
- Horizontal and vertical role relationships defined
- Role purposes that are aligned to the value creation process
- The work of all roles tied to the common planning process
- All roles supplied with access to the process measures for the end-to-end process and everyone involved will understand how their role contributes to performance

43. Customer relationship accountabilities are established in role descriptions

Winning organisations recognise that value is defined by the customer and that long-term success is intrinsically related to understanding and responding to changing customer requirements. Customer relationship accountabilities need to be clearly specified in role descriptions. Customer information is a key input into the planning and improvement systems.

Winning organisations understand the customers' perspective on how satisfied they are with the products that they paid for. It is important to understand how the customer feels emotionally about the organisation supplying the products. It's critical to establish formal and informal feedback systems that are reviewed and acted upon in a timely manner. Customers are people and they need to be listened to and respected.

Example:

A chemical supply organisation was looking to increase the supply contract to a major customer. In the negotiations, the customer introduced concerns regarding material handling of some materials at some of the sites.

The supply organisation produced data that showed all the products were within specification limits upon shipment. The customer became irate with the supplier as he felt that the supplier was in denial as to the problem.

How the customer was feeling became more important than the specification data. Eventually, the supplier began to listen more, to ask more questions and began trying to identify possible causes. The customer now began to feel that the supplier was listening and was engaged in solving the problems. Negotiations were back on track.

The material handling problems were due to how some of the customer sites stored and used the material. The supplier eventually gained more supply and a new service role in assisting sites in the correct management of stock.

In this example, the supplier increased the level of integration into the customer process, increased margin by adding value and improved the perception of the organisation as problem solvers.

44. Standard jobs are approved within limits by the authorised person

Winning organisations require standard jobs to be developed and followed within the limits set by the role accountable for the cost and benefit of the work. Standard jobs allow processes to trigger services to the quality and quantity determined by the authorised person. This empowers the person doing the job and they provide a clear best practice method that can be confidently applied.

Vision and strategy sets the overall boundary conditions for what the organisation will or not consider. Confused or complicated vision and strategy is likely to lead to wider limits and result in more effort being directed into areas of low value to the organisation.

Effective leaders in winning organisations pursue clarity in communication and task assignment while delegating the appropriate discretion and control to their team. Clear outputs, measures and limits that, if reached, trigger feedback to the leader, allows the right people to do the right work at the right time.

Developing standard jobs reduces duplication, shares best practice, respectfully allows the people doing the jobs to own the work and allows the authorising person to focus on improvement work, confidently knowing they will have the opportunity to exercise their discretion if a limit is reached.

Example:

In a metal refining business, the president of the organisation had access to the control panel used by the shift control room to manage the process. From time to time, he called up the control room to discuss trends he was concerned about.

The control room operators felt that the president did not trust them and felt micro-managed. It was suggested that rather than randomly intervene, it might be better to define key process boundary limits that, if breached, would trigger notification to the next level leader. This proved effective in reducing the frequency of random calls with no action, created greater confidence in the control room operators and allowed the president more time to work on longer-term improvement.

Standard jobs can discover unplanned situations and when this occurs, the person involved needs to be clear on what the sponsor for the job wants them to do. Having clear limits takes away the risk and uncertainty of the person making the decision.

45. Standard work routines for the organisation (including key communication and planning meetings) are established

Standard work routines are used in winning organisations to efficiently organise how the people interact in routine communication, planning and decision requirements. Standard work routines allow the organisation to develop a rhythm, a confident predictability that ensures the right people are in the right place at the right time.

Standard work routines include daily, weekly, monthly, quarterly and annual cycles. It is usually the case that the roles closest to the process will have most of their time allocated to work routines and the most senior leaders will have around a quarter of their time allocated to standard work routines.

Optimisation of work routines is part of the planning process and requires review, learning and improvement based upon the measurement of how well a routine is achieving its purpose.

Example:

Performance in a manufacturing organisation was improved by around 20% after a standard meeting that reviewed process performance and tracked priority tasks was introduced. Prior to the standard meeting different people from different departments contacted the supervisor in an ad-hoc fashion, with at times a queue outside the office.

Standardisation quickly provided attendees with a progress update and critical tasks tracked on a whiteboard. Having maintenance, engineering and broader management in attendance contributed to better decision-making and alignment. Longer-term tasks were captured and tracked at weekly and monthly intervals. The whiteboard allowed anyone who could not attend the meeting to quickly come up to speed.

The main driver of improvement was the faster completion of critical tasks.

Standard work also includes building time for leaders to observe the process in action into the schedule and to see how work is being executed. It is difficult to establish the required standard work routines if the processes themselves are out of control.

Organisations can get into a crisis mode of chasing breakdowns and reacting to noise to the point that roles become overloaded and only the urgent short-term work gets done rather than the important high-value work. If this is occurring, an intervention is required.

The most critical first step for an organisation is to realise when it is operating out of control and to understand that being in a reactive mode does not have to be the normal state. Being constantly in reaction mode can be a common trap for leaders who are always busy fighting fires and making decisions on the run. In this situation, their daily schedule is set for them by unplanned events and not by them in a planned manner.

The leader can feel like the hero saving the day every day in this scenario. However, this mode of operation will not achieve continuous improvement. Often an intervention or timeout is required to re-set the priorities for leaders in this situation and to break what is a non-virtuous cycle.

When designing the standard work of a role it is important not to plan to more than 70% of the available time for leaders. It is the leader's role to engage people. The time required to effectively communicate can vary considerably from person to person and situation to situation.

46. Systems are defined, flowcharted and key roles and accountabilities allocated

Systems are owned by the leadership in winning organisations. They are defined with a clear purpose, flowcharts, measures, controls and role accountabilities.

Systems must be owned at the right level in the organisation and this is typically at senior manager level. Only senior managers have the breadth of scope in their role required to understand where the system should start and end, how it fits with other systems, who needs to be involved and what systems will no longer be required or will need modification.

Example:

A group of senior managers in an organisation, having been involved in a discussion on 'what is a system?' were asked to take some time to design a simple system (how to make coffee). Over two hours later the facilitator came back to see a blank page.

Conceptually designing a system is not difficult. However, it is time-consuming work and it takes time to get the system defined clearly and simply. Most of the systems being used in organisations are poorly designed. It is important for leaders to understand that it is their job to plan, develop work routines and provide effective systems.

Example:

In a global resource-based organisation, it was decided by senior leaders to improve the capability of the organisation to execute work more effectively. The organisation had work management systems. However, they were not rigorously followed. Some work was planned, and some was not. Whether a job required authorisation or not was unclear.

The organisation developed flowcharted systems that defined how tasks would be planned and executed. The design of the system identified what was required by each role at each step.

After completing training, each site set about tracking how well they could follow the system. It took sites over six months before they could consistently comply with the system. One of the critical issues was having the right people with the right skills doing the right work the right way. If a person was to go on leave, sometimes there was no person to backfill the role. Only by defining the system, the role accountabilities and tracking performance was it possible to understand, align and improve how work was managed.

To learn efficiently requires the ability to develop theory, apply that theory, measure, analyse and review the results after applying the theory. If the system is not clear or it is not clear how well a system was followed, then it is possible that false conclusions will be made about the effectiveness of the system.

The SIPOC Model provides a sound framework on which to base system design.

Operational Excellence

Figure 19: Winning Organisation Model's operational excellence characteristics

DESIGNING

47. SIPOC Model is understood and applied
48. Management of change is rigorously applied to ensure risk is managed to an acceptable level and improvement will be sustained.
49. Organisation invests in research and the application of leading technology in high value opportunities
50. The organisation has access to the expertise required for designing experiments or undertaking complex projects

MEASURING

51. Minimum output measures are run charted and data guides decision
52. Process managers understand that control of variation at the input and in-process stages will lead to the least variation in outputs
53. Effective systems provide employees with the information needed.

CONTROLLING

54. It is understood that all variation is waste and it is the role of process managers to control variation within acceptable limits
55. Process managers utilise cause and effect maps to build process control capability that ensure root causes are understood
56. Whenever a process intervention is decided the supporting theory is defined and captured
57. Process managers understand the impact of cumulative variation in processes

Operational excellence is the efficient, reliable and profitable operation of the right processes to create products that a customer pays for. It requires the commitment to improve process performance by eliminating waste and designing more effective processes.

The purpose of effective leadership, organisational effectiveness and value focus is to influence the design and operation of processes to create the value required faster, cheaper and better.

Winning organisations align their effort onto the few high-leverage opportunities to improve how processes create value.

The design of the right process and operating it with the least variation will deliver the value required. Processes take inputs and transform them into outputs. The transformation stage is where value is created.

Designing

Operational excellence requires that processes are designed to efficiently transform the right inputs into outputs that the customer wants to buy. Customer desires and expectations change over time and so will the products and the processes making them.

Technology changes and innovation can lead to new, better and faster ways to achieve the same functional objectives. Winning organisations focus on value. They seek better ways to create it by eliminating waste in how processes are operated and designed.

47. SIPOC Model is understood and applied

Winning organisations understand how value is created by processes via the Supplier-Inputs-Process Transformation-Outputs-Customer Model.

SIPOC Model

SIPOC is a standard model used in mapping processes or in describing steps within processes.

The SIPOC Model has been used to describe and design processes in Six Sigma and Lean Manufacturing. It first appeared in mainstream businesses as part of the Total Quality Management (TQM) programs that were prominent in the 1980s.

SIPOC stands for Suppliers, Inputs, Process, Outputs, Customer. It can be used to define who, what, where and how in relation to how value is created from a process.

S I P O C   Model

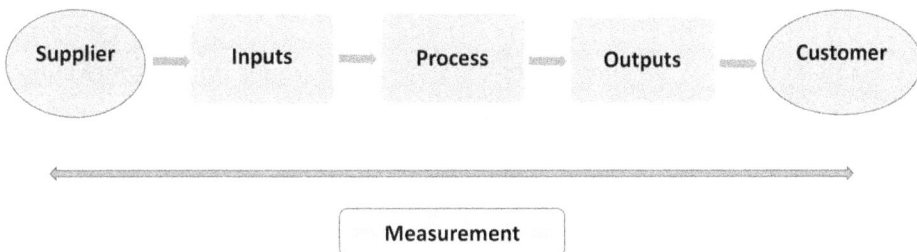

Figure 20: SIPOC Model

The understanding and focus on reducing variation and improving processes is essential to operational excellence. The SIPOC Model is useful in explaining how suppliers need to interact with processes that transform inputs into outputs that the customer wants to pay for.

The **S**upplier provides **I**nputs to the **P**rocess that transforms or transports **O**utputs to a **C**ustomer.

To control a process requires measures and control actions. This ensures variations in inputs, in-process transformations and outputs are kept within the limits specified. Tight control of outputs is a function of the control of input and in-process variation. SIPOC highlights the importance of relationships with the supplier and customer.

Processes add value from transforming inputs into outputs. Arguably, transporting inputs from a supplier to a customer also adds value because customers pay for this. However, if the customer could avoid transport costs, they would.

Operational excellence implies that performance will be improved over time. The objective is to maximise the utilisation of assets to produce the required output better, faster and cheaper. SIPOC provides a model for defining and capturing ideas that can be subsequently analysed, prioritised and then supplied to the planning process.

48. Management of change is rigorously applied to ensure risk is managed at an acceptable level and improvement will be sustained

Winning organisations manage change effectively. There is always risk associated with any action. The effective management of change minimises the unintended consequences from actions and minimises the duplication of effort by ensuring gains made are sustainably locked in.

To ensure a change is sustained, changes must be captured in: specifications, process control, documentation, training and management systems.

Every action taken to improve a process involves change. Changes in one stage of a process can have impacts in other stages. Sometimes a change to improve one stage of a process can have unintended negative consequences elsewhere in the process. It's critical to limit the number of changes being made at any one time to achieve high rates of continuous improvement.

These things are critical to continuous improvement:

- Seeking to understand cause and effect relationships in processes
- Clearly defined projects
- The effective implementation of chosen projects
- The review of results achieved from projects implemented
- Locking in gains

If you make two changes at the same time, how would you know which change had what effect?

Operational excellence requires effective systems to ensure the risks associated with change are kept to an acceptable level and that the changes are robustly supported by systems, standards, training and records. This ensures no unexpected surprises from making a change and ensures that risks of an unwanted negative effect from a change are controlled to an acceptable level.

Example:

A goods receiving department was experiencing congestion, difficulty in finding goods received and difficulty in reliably turning over goods within a certain time.

The area supervisor mapped the existing process and then made changes to organise the goods receiving process and ensure everything was processed in chronological order. He was able to improve the process quite quickly.

The supervisor then had to take an extended leave of absence. Unfortunately, there was no documentation, work routines or training that described the process changes he had made and the store gradually descended into chaos once again.

You need to consider how to lock in the benefits and avoid unintended negative consequences well before the execution phase.

Example:

Marketing identified the potential to make a higher value product from an existing processing plant by blending in additional feed material to increase the overall product grade. The higher grade meant higher premiums and more profit. After a short trial, the organisation committed to the change.

However, the additional feed material behaved differently in the process plant and an increased level of dust began to occur. The plant was not designed to handle the finer material. The dust created health and safety problems and additional cost to clean up and maintain the equipment.

In this example, the management of the change process was not completed thoroughly before committing to the change.

49. Organisation invests in research and the application of leading technology in high-value opportunities

The leadership of winning organisations understand that learning and innovation is critical to improving faster than the competition. Equally as important is the ability to focus learning and innovation onto high-value priorities.

Winning organisations invest in research and apply new technology to high-value opportunities. The effort is always value-focused and reviewed alongside other discretionary opportunities.

Technology can enable step change in capability to create value. It takes time for new technology to be proven and for it to become reliable. The organisation must understand how new technology will be implemented in ways that all stakeholders believe positively reflect the core values of the organisation. It is often the case that consideration of implications of core values and ethics is the most time consuming and complex step when embracing new technology.

Effective management of change is critical to balancing risk and reward. The rate of technological development is now faster than ever. Winning organisations invest in research, networking and the implementation of technology in high-leverage areas. The willingness to accept the risk in pursuing new technology is considered against the estimated value that may be gained.

Resources must be invested, to research, develop and test new ways of doing things. It's essential to engage in the appropriate use of the right technology in the right way at the right time.

Leading edge technology can be expensive to acquire or develop. Only when the organisation has a clear understanding of the process to which the technology will be applied should investments be made.

There are at least as many stories of failures in the rapid adoption of a new technology as there are stories of success. Risks with new technology are not just technical in nature. The implications on people and how they will feel about the technology can be significant.

The use of technology can be highly effective in reducing variation provided that the process is stable and controlled. A simple example is driving a car at a determined speed limit. In this case the driver is simply adjusting throttle or braking to maintain the car at a set speed. This task is neither particularly interesting nor sufficiently important for it to remain the focus of the conscious human mind for very long. People can concentrate on more than a single feedback loop and so become distracted. For this reason, the variation in speed of a person driving will be wider than that of a dedicated computer.

The work of people in a winning organisation today will not be the same in ten years' time. The organisation will have developed new knowledge, reduced variation and applied technology to the highest leverage areas within the business.

People are an expensive resource and technology has been progressively replacing the highly repetitive work that people have been doing for many years. The technology will soon be reliable enough to replace driving roles in our society completely. The most significant challenges to this change will occur with how the change affects people.

People are great at devising tools and methods and innovating. They thrive on finding out how to get something done. People are the vital resource in winning organisations that generate new ideas, find new solutions and build the values driven culture.

Example:

An automotive parts manufacturing plant produced a sintered sprocket part. During the sintering process, a rough ridge occurred on the sprocket that had to be removed before sale. To remove the ridge, they used a de-burring tool that was pushed through each sprocket several times until the burr was removed.

It was decided that this would be a batch job done on day shift. Each day there would be a 44-gallon drum of sprockets for someone to de-burr. The supervisor would typically give this job to the least popular person in the crew as a punishment. Not only was it mind-numbingly boring, it also gave the employee a sore wrist and hand after an hour. People hated it and would use all their intellect and ingenuity to get out of doing the task.

Almost miraculously, one day a new employee moved onto the de-burring job and refused to be taken off it. From then on, only this person did this job. I have only ever seen this once in my working career, where a person could remain content doing such a repetitive task that requires little intellectual capability. There is always an exception to every rule and this individual was a remarkable exception.

Most people need a certain amount of intellectual challenge in their work and if the organisation is not providing it, people find other ways to use their intellect. Employees who are given work well below their intellectual

capability often make their own entertainment. If this situation is left to go on for too long the entertainment can include testing the boss, trying a few different things to see what happens, testing whether anyone notices if we don't do this, staying in the lunchroom longer so we can talk about what we will do outside of work. All these things can be symptomatic of a lack of interesting brain work.

Apart from not deriving the benefit gained from using the intellectual capability of employees to improve the business, it is almost certain that wasted intellectual effort will end up being used to the detriment of the organisation. Technology that is applied to reduce the need for people to do highly repetitive and low skill tasks frees up the time of employees to focus on the next improvement.

Winning organisations have a clear technological investment target that may be expressed as a percentage of profits or a set provision of funds.

Winning organisations that demonstrate this characteristic will:

- Understand their high-value priorities
- Be engaged in innovation and research in high-value areas
- Implement leading technology in priority value-creating areas
- Have leaders who actively encourage learning and innovation within the organisation
- Have leaders who understand the importance of core values and ethics in managing technological change

50. The organisation has access to the expertise required for designing experiments or undertaking complex projects

Winning organisations recognise that not all expertise needs to exist within the organisation. People don't know what they don't know. You must ensure that they have access to the required expertise for experimental design or in guiding the organisation through complex projects. It is often preferable to use an external expert resource for infrequent complex design work. This is likely to be more cost effective and deliver higher quality outcomes, as a specialist is likely to have expert level of proficiency in the field.

A Place for Lean Six Sigma?

Organisations sometimes ask, 'Is it better to implement Lean Manufacturing or Six Sigma?'

Often organisations that have undertaken a Lean or Six Sigma initiative are left disappointed or even cite that the methods do not work. The reality is that Lean and Six Sigma offer excellent best practice methods. However, these are methods and tools that only create value if they assist the organisation to execute the high value opportunities faster, better and cheaper.

Organisations that start Lean or Six Sigma initiatives without first establishing what the organisation is trying to achieve or how this new initiative fits with other initiatives, tend to get a poor return on investment. Success along the journey to becoming a winning organisation requires aligned effort through effective leadership across value-focus, operational excellence and organisational effectiveness to achieve the vision, goals and objectives.

Lean or Six Sigma is not a strategy. Comments such as 'we are doing lean' by senior leaders are a virtual death kiss to success. What is being inferred by such comments is that the program itself is the goal and this is too ambiguous.

Any program, as with good ideas, must be assessed against the goals of the business and considered through the planning, analysis and scheduling disciplines.

I would consider it to be best practice to ensure that some people in the organisation have knowledge and competency in best practice methods such as Lean Six Sigma. This allows the organisation access to knowledge of best practice theory and methods that may be appropriate at some time.

Having access to a good toolkit is one thing. However, you still need to know what tool to use and when. Most improvement opportunities do not require

complex statistical analysis. On occasions, however, well-designed factorial experiments may be required, and advanced statistical analysis may reveal new information from data that would otherwise remain hidden. Hence, it's important to develop the right level of knowledge and competence in certain roles.

Measuring

It is only through measurement that a process can be managed. If you want to achieve the low levels of variation necessary to be a winning organisation it's essential to understand the variability of input materials and services, the variation of in-process transformation processes effecting the outputs delivered to and paid for by the customer.

No single measure can be used to fully understand a process. It's important to establish the right suite of measures to guide timely decision-making so you can achieve the controls necessary for a highly predictable process performance.

Lean and Learning to See

All organisations need to understand the concept of value and waste. Any effort expended in producing a product that is not required and paid for by the customer is waste. Effort expended in increasing value through improving processes is done in the expectation that there will be a future return on that effort.

All variation is waste. Not all waste has the same value, though. Waste that causes constraints or bottlenecks in key processes is likely to be the most valuable area for you to focus on improvement.

All processes have variation. The work of all process managers is to manage the variation that has the greatest impact on value. A process manager's role is to ensure that the variation is controlled within the limits required to deliver value to the customer.

There are only two ways that processes create value:

- Transformation—where inputs are made into the outputs paid for by a customer
- Transportation—value is created by paid transportation inputs from a supply location to the customer's location. Note: When considering the economy of scale and relative cost impact of transportation on overall costs there is often value in transportation.

Variation in processes or adding steps that the customer does not pay for is waste. For example, delivering an item to the customer from the supplier's warehouse more than once would be a clear waste step. There will always be variation and at any given time, the manager will focus effort on the variation that impacts value the most. The variation of concern could be adding costs, impacting process throughput, slowing down the process or adversely impacting quality or people.

The principle that all variation is waste and all processes have variation must be understood. All employees must understand that all roles with process management authority must reduce or eliminate waste having an impact on value.

It is surprising how often managers argue that not all variation is wasteful. Some managers strongly believe that some variation is useful, as new learning is born from variation. However, it is far more effective to conduct a properly designed experiment than wait for patterns of variation to verify a new theory. While all variation is waste, the manager must still ensure that the value generated in reducing variation justifies the investment.

No matter how tightly a process is controlled there will always be variation. Just imagine a polished knife edge that looks smooth to the naked eye, if you look at the edge under a magnifying glass and discover it's rough and scratched. Whether it would be worthwhile using a laser sharpening tool on the knife depends on whether a better knife edge improves value more than the cost of laser sharpening.

The fastest rate of improvement is achieved by using the Pareto principle to focus on only the few things that create the greatest value. Any idea for improvement should always be assessed from a cost-benefit perspective. This is achieved by adopting an expansive initial survey of all solutions and then, in an iterative fashion, refining and tuning solutions to find the best overall value option.

Sometimes managers attempt to implement a step change to a process that is statistically out of control (meaning that it is not possible to predict the likely output of the process in the future). When variation is random and sits outside the limits of two standard deviations of the mean, the process is deemed to be statistically out of control.

A process must be in statistical control before attempting to make step changes. Step change is intended to shift the capability of the process. If attempting to make a step change when the process is already behaving unpredictably (out

of control) then it is impossible to be certain whether future process change was caused by the planned action or some other random action.

The use of control charts is essential to understand whether a process in control or not. Control charts help to understand whether a result is likely to be common (something happening on a regular basis) or special (something new impacting the process). The use of charts is an important first step in learning to see the variation occurring in the process. The use of control charts allows the manager to determine whether a data point is likely to be considered normal behaviour for the process or whether it represents a change that needs some corrective action. A process that is in control may still exhibit high variation, but the pattern of variation has a high degree of confidence of falling between the control limits.

When the customer specification requires outcomes that fall outside the range of the normal performance of a process, a change in the capability of the process is required

In setting goals, the process manager must understand that all variation is waste and that their work is to eliminate or reduce the waste. The use of data in decision-making and performance tracking (in at least run chart form) is important in understanding variation and process capability.

Operational excellence requires process managers to look at the right data in chart format to see and control variation. Once they can see the real variation, managers immediately begin asking questions and form hypotheses as to causes of variation which is fundamental to continuous improvement.

Control Limits

A process is said to be in control when the data point sits within the pattern of results that it has delivered over time. It is usual for control limits to be set at a level that includes 95% of process data excluding known special cause event data (two standard deviations in normal distribution).

By using control limits the manager has a high degree of certainty that there is a discrete and special change to the process if a data point falls outside the control limit. In such instances, there is a high likelihood that there is some cause that is not part of the usual performance of the process.

In this case, the manager is looking for a special cause. This is likely to be a specific and a discrete event with a specific time of occurrence. The earlier that the process trend data can alert the manager of a change, the more likely it is that the manager will be able to identify the special cause.

When seeking to improve processes that are in control the manager is looking to understand common causes of variation. Common causes occur within the normal process, so they have been occurring in the historical data at some frequency.

Common causes of variation are implicit in how the current systems, inputs, process set points and environmental factors have operated in the past. Systematically eliminating or reducing the causes of variation leads to not only more predictable performance but higher average performance.

Six Sigma offers excellent statistical tools to improve an organisation's ability to understand variation. However, in most cases, simple run charting and setting of control limits will be sufficient for process managers to be able to see and act appropriately to improve the process performance.

Using run charts and control charts is extremely important in ensuring that there is only intervention when there is a reason to do so.

Example:

In a mining organisation that had become accustomed to reporting tables of data presented as averages over shifts, days, weeks and months, the manager decided to simply look at the raw data from 12-hour shift intervals.

The manager was shocked by the large swings in performance that were now visibly obvious. He began to see patterns as he dug into the data. There was a realisation that much of the variation was being initiated by management interventions intended to increase production at the end of weekly and monthly reporting intervals. Record high production was consistently followed by periods of low production.

The manager could now see the high variation as waste. He decided to stop pushing for new records and instead focused on reducing variation. His courage in making such a change in behaviour was not easy.

The focus away from records to reducing variation resulted in an overall improved average performance. Even more powerfully, it resulted in the organisation being able to see what was really going on in the process through use of run charts. This helped the managers to understand that improving performance was achieved by getting processes under control and by reducing variation, as opposed to pushing for new record maximums.

An example of a run chart and histogram is below (reference Vale Inco)

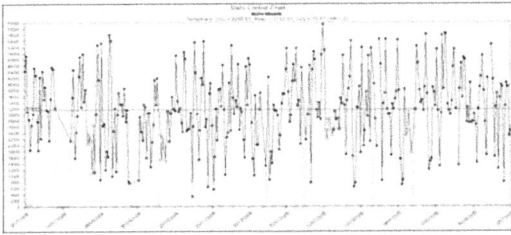

Figure 21: Example of run chart

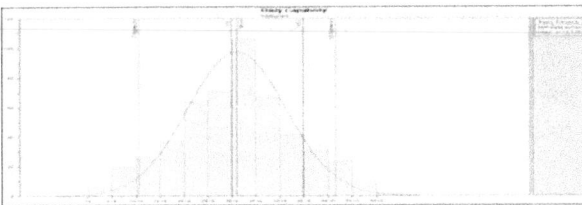

Figure 22: Example of histogram

It is necessary to understand that the purpose of measurement is to guide the manager's decision as to when to make a process intervention. Basic run charting with control limits allows the manager to determine when an intervention is required. Note that the term 'manager' is being applied to be the person accountable for the control of a process.

It is important to look at the right measures—those where there is a direct and easily understood correlation of the measure to the purpose or goal. There are three types of measures within a process (SIPOC Model): input, in process and output measures. Often managers only focus on output measures.

To minimise variation effectively, managers must also be focused on the control of variation at in-process and input stages. For example, if while seeking to manage your personal expenditures you only look at the monthly credit card statement, this is a less effective way of managing expenses than scrutinising commitments at the purchasing stage.

Minimum Output Measures

You cannot manage something that you do not measure. This is a simple and obvious reality. However, managers often struggle to establish the right measures. Organisations can be flooded with data which creates noise, confusion, wasted time and resources. Many organisations lack the discipline to determine what really needs to be measured, and in the worst cases, the organisation becomes confused by creating indices that few people even understand.

Example:

One government organisation was driven by a measure called MOHRI. Most managers knew that MOHRI related to headcount; few knew that MOHRI was short for 'Mandatory Obligatory Human Resources Indicator'. This indicator counted employees paid for a given period, although it excluded and double-counted people depending on what pay classification they were assigned to.

In this organisation, individual employee payment adjustments were entered manually into a system from forms submitted to a centralised payroll group. The processing of forms was on average about six weeks behind. At any one time, it was not possible for managers to reconcile accurately the MOHRI reported number to actual headcount. If MOHRI was above target a review would be requested. However, it was not possible in many cases for the accountable manager to reconcile discrepancies.

Such measures should be avoided in favour of simple metrics that can be easily understood and preferably represented graphically. In this case the number of full-time equivalents would have been a more effective measure.

There is another problem when data is collected and not used regularly to guide decisions. The data becomes corrupted. Errors in entry, calibration and correlation with other measures and events occur that make the historical data useless.

What are the right measures? In answering this question, it is helpful to define a clear purpose for measurement - to provide the information required for the manager to know when to make an intervention. Given that all processes will have some variation, the measure needs to have set trigger points or control limits that if reached, require the manager to take an action to move the process back into the acceptable performance range.

A key component of Six Sigma methods is focused on understanding process information and the utilisation of statistical methods to provide greater certainty as to whether the process is really changing or whether the variation is part of the normal performance. The process manager needs to be able to attribute a performance change with the cause before deciding any corrective action. Managers who make changes without understanding the normal variation in the process can exacerbate variation and in doing so, make the process performance worse.

In determining whether to make a change it is important that the manager understand whether the process is statistically in control or not. When a process is statistically in control he/she can be confident of the likelihood of future outputs falling within the control limits. A process would be out of control if the range of outcomes cannot be predicted to fall within the control limits.

Introducing change into a process that is out of control will mean that the manager cannot be certain if a subsequent outcome is caused by the intended change or some other unknown effect.

Winning organisations expend the least amount of effort to achieve their goals and objectives. No single measure can completely describe any process. An action can have beneficial effects in one area and negative consequences in other areas that need to be understood. There is a minimum suite of output measures that are required to adequately describe the performance of any process (reference: Vale Inco AMF).

Time: What is the percentage of available calendar time that the process/organisation operated? Time can relate to the services delivered to the customer or to utilisation of equipment.

Rate: How many output units were achieved per unit of time from the process?

Quality: What percentage of output met the required customer specifications?

Cost: What was the cost per unit of output?

Reliability: How many unscheduled interventions occurred per unit of time?

Risk: What are considered the highest risk issues that could affect the process/organisation's ability to continue to perform as it has done in the past?

The absence of one or more of these output metrics will result in the manager not having complete visibility of the required data that describes process performance. Actions that may affect one of the measures can impact others. For example, not doing maintenance will allow more time to operate in the short term. However, not doing maintenance may affect other measures including risk and reliability over the longer term.

Example:

If a person does not complete a service on their automobile, then they will not experience the loss of its availability and will not incur the immediate cost of the service. The trade-offs from not doing the service are potential reliability issues, an increased risk of breakdown or deteriorating efficiency and a higher cost of repair when the automobile does break down.

There are also critical input measures that directly relate to the output measures. Examples include:

Time: Maintenance downtime, breakdowns, manning shortages

Rate: Percentage of maximum sustainable rate (MSR), climate, seasonal factors such as weather

Quality: Health, safety and environment measures, waste, specifications of input materials and services, having the right people in the right roles at the right time

Reliability: Compliance with planned work, alarm conditions

Cost: Cost of services, re-work, input materials and services

Risk: Climate, community, plant integrity, market

It is important that when prioritising where to assign resources that the full suite of minimum measures be considered so you can make the most informed decision. In the automobile service option, if only short-term availability and cost were considered, then the decision would be to not service the automobile. Only when understanding the implications over a longer period does the service emerge as the preferred option.

To assist decision-making processes on priorities, it's essential to have a standard analysis tool that will provide a consistent and valid method of evaluating and prioritising tasks or projects. These tools should clearly define options, the impact to the business and an estimation of the risk or degree of certainty of each option delivering the estimated outcomes.

A common trap is to focus only on costs and production and not appreciate changes in quality, reliability and risk. This trap features in most major disasters, particularly regarding gradual unappreciated increases in the level of risk as controls are eroded as people chase production and cost. Then the disaster occurs and the leadership is exposed to a stack of contributing factors that have their root cause in not always considering the implications of actions over the full suite of measures.

51. Minimum output measures are run-charted and data guides decision-making

Winning organisations always seek data to inform decision-making and increase the confidence level in estimating the outcome from each action. They appreciate the need to understand variation using run charts.

Minimum output measures exist that include:

Time: What is the percentage of available calendar time that the process operated?

Rate: How many output units were achieved per unit of time from the process?

Quality: What percentage of output met the required customer specifications?

Cost: What was the cost per unit of output?

Reliability: How many unscheduled interventions occurred per unit of time?

Risk: What are the critical failure scenarios that may impact the process's ability to continue to perform as it has done in the past?

Winning organisations understand that there are a minimum set of output measures that must be considered together to fully understand process performance. They know that a decision to make a change is likely to affect more than one measure.

For example, in any process that uses machinery that needs maintenance, deferring it will increase time and potential production in the short term. This strategy will eventually impact other measures, such as reliability. Deferring maintenance may immediately increase the risk level.

Example:

The focus for paying bonuses in a mine was on tonnes per month (time and rate). If production quantity was running behind the monthly target the mine would push almost anything it could down the ore chute in an attempt to catch up the deficit. The mill would complain about tramp steel, large rocks and out of specification quality feed toward the end of the month. In this example a lack of consistent focus on quality was the problem. Often the mill would then suffer downtime early in the following month due to damage from tramp steel and the impact of lower grade ore.

Example:

Improved short-term reliability of a large reactor was achieved by widening the range of operating temperatures the process could experience before tripping. This increased the risk of overpressure in the vessel. Only by understanding the risk associated with this change could the full process implications be understood.

Example:

Reliability was improved by disconnecting the temperature trip on a large engine. Only by understanding the risk associated with the change could a complete picture be gleaned.

Example:

Less expensive fuel was chosen for vehicles to reduce operating costs. There was a need to understand the impact on reliability and risk to fully understand the implications of this change

52. Process managers understand that control of variation at the input and in-process stages will lead to the least variation in outputs

Winning organisations understand that to achieve the least variability in output measures requires effective controls at the input and in-process stage. Output measures ultimately define value. However, relying on signals from output measures alone leads to delays in control actions and more variation and waste.

At any point in a process, the variation that you see and measure represents the cumulative effect of variation that has occurred during the prior steps. Time adds further complexity to understanding the cause of variation. Output measures always have time lag and this can result in the decay and corruption of data relating to the cause of variation.

If you have ever been surprised by a monthly report indicating an over-spend and then had to go back and truly find out why, then you will understand how difficult it can be to find a cause. When looking at the monthly report, a manager reported that the reason the costs were over-plan was due to a major overhaul on a truck. When asked, 'Does that mean that the overhaul was planned for later and annual costs are still on track?' he did not know. The manager needed to know the reason the overhaul was carried out at that time before he could make any valid judgement on the implications to the overall budget.

53. Effective systems provide employees with the information needed

Winning organisations understand the need for employees to make decisions in a timely manner within defined boundary limits. Effective systems are required to ensure employees have the information required to support effective decision-making when they require it.

Winning organisations must learn. Connecting people to knowledge and developing the behaviours of ask-learn-share in some form are essential to access the full range of knowledge available. It's essential to have a system that is understood and can be accessed by all employees.

The systems don't need to be complex or expensive but the ability to easily conduct searches to find the right information must be a feature.

Today, social media is becoming a fast and powerful medium for large numbers of people (and activist groups) to develop a voice and exert significant influence over organisations and governments. Winning organisations must embrace these forums and learn how to use them effectively in their knowledge management and communication systems.

The internet has profoundly changed the way people communicate and how they live. It has been estimated that the average amount of time people spend on Facebook alone is six hours per week (and rising at a rapid rate).

Facebook now has the most comprehensive demographic database in the world and using well-designed analytics can measure and categorise people in ways that were not previously feasible. With something like six million postings a minute on Facebook it is fast becoming the preferred vehicle for advertising.

Most organisations are just scratching the surface in how well they are leveraging the internet. Any winning organisation needs to explore how best to use the internet as part of their technology investment.

Established bricks-and-mortar organisations have a major challenge as they compete with new digital network-based organisations that can be nimble, accept risk more readily and can utilise the capability of people more effectively to provide lower cost and more personalised service to customers.

Controlling

Nothing is certain in how a process will perform. Changes can occur at any stage and at any time. It is through measurement that process managers can determine where and when a change occurs.

All processes will have some variation. Process management involves a series of controls that respond to measurement signals to instigate a corrective action. A level of problem-solving capability is required by the process manager to determine cause and effect relationships. This helps with deciding the most effective response when a process measure moves outside established control limits.

Winning organisations seek to keep their processes within the control limits required to achieve the specified process performance.

54. It is understood that all variation is waste and it is the process managers role to control variation within acceptable limits

Winning organisations understand that variation is waste. Process managers understand their roles in controlling variation within acceptable limits.

All employees are engaged in seeking to minimise variation including how work is planned and executed. All employees need to understand that variation is waste and variations in what people do is a major contributor to process variability. Consider the variation in the actions of people and then standardise. It is always more cost effective to ensure that the variation in people's actions is examined before diving too much into process data analysis.

Even though simple control charts will be sufficient for controlling most processes, 'you don't know what you don't know'. It is essential for winning organisations to have a learning culture with access to expertise in leading methods such as Lean Six Sigma if required.

For example, Six Sigma provides excellent guidance in the design of valid experiments that could be invaluable when needed to determine valid cause and effect relationships between multiple variables.

Example:

In a smelter process, one shift would operate the furnace at as low an energy input as they could to ensure that the integrity of the furnace refractory was protected by a frozen flux layer. The relieving shift operated the furnace at an elevated power input to ensure that the furnace feed and the molten metal extraction could be performed with minimal difficulty.

There were two different operating strategies for the same furnace that changed every 12 hours. This drove considerable process variation (waste). Neither shift was doing anything completely wrong. However, the root cause was that there was no written standard operating procedure.

An interesting and emotional exchange occurred when they developed a standard operating procedure. After implementing the standard procedure, the variation in output measures disappeared, as did the emotional tension with the process operating with less variation and the integrity of the refractory preserved.

It's critical to establish effective measures that guide decision-making in order to control processes and gain continuous improvement. No single measure can adequately describe a process. Controlling variation at the input and in-process stages is essential to achieving the least waste in the outputs for customers. How data is collected and used in decision-making is an important consideration of leaders.

55. Process managers utilise cause and effect maps to understand root causes

Winning organisations seek to understand cause and effect relationships to improve process control. The use of root cause analysis allows them to focus effort in an effective and efficient manner.

The use of fishbone (cause and effect) diagrams *(A Guide to Quality Control* by Dr K Ishikawa) provides a simple and effective way to understand what factors (causes) impact the output (effects).

There can be many causes that contribute to an event occurring. It can be difficult to decide on where to prioritise your effort to prevent the reoccurrence of an unwanted event. To become a winning organisation, effort must be prioritised to address the cause/s that are having the greatest impact.

Root cause analysis was developed by NASA in the 1950s. It is the preferred method for ensuring that efforts are prioritised to addressing causes that prevent a particular event from reoccurring. Root cause analysis tests whether a cause, if eliminated, would prevent the event from occurring again in the future.

The concept of root cause analysis is widely understood. The ability to determine that a cause is truly a root cause requires a level of rigour and validation that is not as common.

When considering cause and effect, tools like fishbone diagrams provide a useful structure to summarise process knowledge. Operationally excellent organisations understand the value of identifying and addressing root causes as it prevents wasted effort and rework.

There are always many contributing factors in any event. Eliminating these does not ensure that the event cannot recur. A root cause when addressed, breaks the sequence of events with certainty. Once again, a clear and concise description of a cause will allow similarly concise assessment as to whether it is a root cause.

The traffic investigation method of developing a step by step time sequence of data is used to analyse an incident. Sometimes there may be conflicting information, and the process of determining a root cause considers what data supports and does not support a certain hypothesis. All root cause analyses require a clear problem statement. A problem statement of "preventing someone from falling from height" is quite different from a statement of "preventing someone dying from a fall from height". The fall arrest harnesses that have become popular are a control intended to address dying from a fall from height. Preventing someone from falling from height would lead to ideas of how to eliminate the potential to fall. Containment of the person within a fixed structure, or preventing the need to be over 2 metres above the ground might address root causes if fall prevention was the consequence of interest. In many processing plants, locating valves near to ground or with secure catwalks is a design feature to eliminate risk of falls. I have seen many situations where people are wearing fall arrest harnesses at height that offer them no protection from serious injury if they fall. In most of these situations if they had been required to seek prevention of falling there were containment solutions that could have reasonably been applied. This highlights the importance of getting the consequence of interest well defined when conducting root cause analysis.

Example:

In a car collision incident, the responsible driver was identified as being under 20 years of age. He had only recently been given a full licence and was estimated to be travelling more than the speed limit as he drove through a red light.

One possible cause could be insufficient training. However, if more training was provided, this would not ensure that the event could not happen again. A root cause in this incident was driving through the red light. Any solution that could prevent driving through a red light would prevent this incident from occurring again.

When investigating an incident or process change it is important to limit the decay or corruption of data by acting quickly. Placing data on a timeline helps you understand the sequence of events when analysing for potential root causes.

There are always multiple root causes. One model suggests that there will be root causes in the areas of: machine, people and environment. It takes time, disciplined data collection and careful evaluation against the factual data (or evidence) to ensure that the root causes have been identified.

In a simple example, a person suffers a minor burn from spilling hot coffee. Possible root causes are that the person did not keep the cup level, the cup contained liquid hot enough to cause a burn, the liquid fell from the cup onto a person and the person was moving. Contributing factors might be that they were rushing, they were distracted by something, the cup was filled higher than normal, the person had light clothing on as it was a warm day, and they were tired.

Only by eliminating at least one root cause can the effect be guaranteed not to occur again. In this example, root cause solutions might include actions that would prevent coffee from being hot enough to cause a burn or prevent material from spilling onto a person.

Many root causes have origins in system deficiencies and hence, the actual sequence of events could have been set in motion even years before the effect manifested itself. Understanding the whole process is important in root cause analysis to ensure the most effective control can be identified.

56. Whenever a process intervention is decided the supporting theory is defined and captured

Winning organisations seek to formulate valid theory to support and guide process control. Theories help explain why cause and effect relationships are valid. Theories provide more confidence in predicting future outcomes than data correlation alone.

A study identified that people who drink red wine a few times a week have a lower risk of heart attack. There are many possibilities as to why the study came up with this finding. It is quite possible that the study itself was not well designed and that there were other factors more significant than wine within the sample populations compared.

The theory proposed was antioxidants in the wine were beneficial. A theory allows for further experiments to be designed to further support or disprove the theory.

In this case, the jury is still out on whether the findings were valid. It seems that red wine consumption was linked in this study to other factors such as access to medical professionals, diet and lifestyle.

There is a simple and effective way to build understanding of a cause and effect outcome called '5 Whys'. You can gain a much deeper understanding of an event by simply asking 'Why?' five times. For example, why did the compressor stop? Because of over-vibration. Why was there over-vibration? The compressor exceeded its speed limit. Why did it exceed the speed limit? Because the compressor was surging. Why was the compressor surging? Because the gas composition was changing. Why was the gas composition changing? Because the water condenser was flooded.

Example:

In laboratory testing, a scientist found that by adding calcium carbonate to a slurry the recovery rates of metal from a certain ore increased. When asked why, the scientist had no theory. When asked what confidence there was that the results from the laboratory testing could be transferred to a large-scale plant the answer was 'I don't know'.

The scientist needed to gain a better understanding of why adding calcium carbonate increased recovery rates in the experiment to improve the confidence that the result would be reproduced on a larger and more expensive scale. Subsequent tests determined that there had been sampling anomalies that led to the original findings and no valid theory was found.

Whether a theory is valid or not, the discipline to define a theory is critical to efficient learning. Well-designed experiments can be executed to determine whether data supports a theory.

57. Process managers understand the impact of cumulative variation in processes

Winning organisations seek more knowledge about cumulative variation, so they can understand value from process interventions better. Understanding cumulative variation helps improve decision-making and helps avoid over-estimating value from changes.

Eliminating or reducing variation in all routine processes contributes to improved performance. It's necessary for process managers to understand how to identify the bottleneck of the process and to understand how addressing the constraint will impact the final outputs that are paid for by the customer.

It's cost-effective to use process simulations. The dice simulation is a simple and effective basic training exercise to help managers appreciate the impacts of variation, bottlenecks and cumulative variation.

Standardisation of what people do helps reduce variation, as does simplification. Removing non-value adding process steps decreases waste and reduces process noise.

Applying WOM

Winning Organisation Model

Figure 23: Winning Organisation Model

At the highest level, WOM reinforces the connection between the four capabilities in everything the organisation does.

If considering committing effort to an area of **organisational effectiveness** the model prompts the following questions:

- What does the leadership need to do?
- How will this effect processes?
- What value will this produce?
- Is this a critical project for the organisation?

- If considering committing effort to an area of **operational excellence** the model prompts the following questions:

    - How will this affect people in the organisation?

    - What does the leadership need to do?

    - What value will this produce?

    - Is it a critical project for us?

If considering committing effort in an area of **value focus** the model prompts the following questions:

- What impact will this have on processes?

- What do leaders need to do?

- How does it affect people?

- What value will this produce?

- Is it a critical project for the organisation?

If considering committing effort in an area of **effective leadership** the model prompts the following questions:

- How does this affect people?

- What impact will this have on the process?

- What value will this produce?

- Is it a critical project for the organisation?

The discipline to work through these questions ensures that the implications of a task or project is always considered across the four capabilities.

WOM provides capabilities and characteristics that any organisation can quickly use as a reference. This helps identifies gaps in thinking or capability that must be addressed if the organisation needs to achieve best in class performance.

WOM seeks to provide the definition and understanding of these characteristics to ensure success. Each characteristic is written in a way that should allow the leadership of any organisation to assess the current capability and then develop a suitable action to close the gap.

Where gaps are identified, the organisation should be able to find a way to close them in a manner that suits their circumstances. There is always more than one way to achieve a characteristic. By evaluating the organisations

capability against the characteristics defined in the WOM the senior leadership will understand what is working well and where the gaps are. Gaps in effective leadership characteristics will usually be a high priority for action, however, trying to do too many things at the same time is a common mistake.

It is always recommended that any organisation focuses effort on the few highest value opportunities. It may take some time before an identified gap leads to a task that is a priority for action. Attempting to address too many gaps at the same time is unlikely to deliver the benefits expected. For example, high employee turnover may be a higher value priority than developing process simulation capability.

Effective leadership will always determine the rate of improvement. Establishing the right thinking is an essential first step in closing gaps.

For each of the essential characteristics summarised below, the organisation will be in one of three states:

1. **Non-compliant**—There is no evidence to support the characteristic being present in the organisation

2. **Partial compliance**—Leadership agrees that the characteristic is one that they are seeking to develop and there is some evidence that supports this

3. **Fully compliant**—The characteristic is desired by the leadership, written into policies and procedures, and stakeholders confirm it is a feature of how the organisation operates

Example:

Essential attribute 1—Senior leaders are committed to pursue clarity in all communications—is put to the senior leadership as a proposition that they are either committed to or not. If not, the assessment is complete and the organisation would be non-compliant for this characteristic.

If the leadership believes they are committed to this characteristic, then they would seek examples of how it is being exercised. If there is written evidence supporting the characteristic, then the organisation would be at least partially compliant in this characteristic.

If the leadership felt the organisation past the partial compliance step, the next stage is to test whether stakeholders such as investors, customers, employees and possibly community representatives believe that the organisation demonstrates this characteristic. If the evidence (survey

results) supports it being a characteristic, then the organisation would be fully compliant for this characteristic.

It is possible, but unusual, for the leadership to reject a characteristic as being applicable to their organisation. If any characteristic is rejected, it is likely that the leadership is not yet ready to pursue a winning organisation objective. This is not necessarily a bad thing, as it may save significant waste in pursuing initiatives that are not consistent with the current organisations vision. Many, many businesses do quite well without ever aspiring to be a winning organisation.

It is better for the current leadership to honestly represent their viewpoint. Saying one thing and demonstrating another is more damaging than simply explaining the basis for not accepting a characteristic as being valid. It is more common for an organisation to recognise a gap in capability rather than dismiss the value of a characteristic.

The leadership should work through each characteristic together and then review their findings. All organisations will have some or even many of the characteristics.

The review begins the process of prioritising areas for idea generation and analysis to develop tasks for consideration in the planning process.

Some people may contend that self-assessment is not valid; that it is too subjective. My experience has been that self-assessment is usually valid when honestly attempted and it is the most cost-effective way for an organisation to assess where it is at.

It is interesting to note that communication is a common organisational weakness cited in organisational surveys. Communication is vital in aligning effort and is key work of leadership. It has been my experience that when the leadership are truly committed to communication they find ways to improve it. Many leaders also do not clearly understand their essential role in achieving the clarity, alignment and collective learning required for the organisation to focus on value.

All organisations will find some evidence of most of the characteristics. Winning organisations will seek to fully develop capability in each characteristic. The larger the organisation, the more difficult it is to achieve complete alignment with stakeholders and there are greater dependencies on well-designed systems and communication/alignment capability.

I believe that most organisations have most of the capabilities to undertake the winning organisation journey using predominantly internal resources. The rate at which they can learn will influence the rate at which they improve. Leadership capability always determines the rate of improvement.

Using external resources in the right areas at the right time can be helpful, however, the leadership cannot be placed into the hands of external resources. A poor presentation delivered by a committed leader is worth much more than a swish presentation delivered by someone external to the organisation. This is because it is only when the leader's commitment and communication is clear and felt, that real sustainable change occurs.

When planning for success, it is critical that competency-based learning is employed and that the leadership confirms that the learning is being translated into the correct actions. Leaders are required to be in the workplace to listen, understand, share and verify that the actions are occurring as intended.

Every level and every silo in the organisation is a point where breakdowns in alignment can and will occur at some time. The goal is for there to be no surprises from the CEO to the floor operator, and this requires sufficient time within the standard work of all roles to be allocated to communication.

If the CEO consistently finds that one team does not understand what is required, then the leader of that team has the problem. However, if the CEO finds that all teams do not understand, then the CEO has the problem. Either way, when there is misalignment, there is likely inefficient prioritisation of resources and a gap in performance.

The identification of any gap requires effort from all levels in alignment that must be planned within the standard work. All steps of the PDCA cycle need to be exercised and action taken to address gaps. Sometimes the corrective action is simply building a better understanding and sometimes it may be to improve a system or even change the priorities of the plan.

There is usually some variation in performance and alignment across various departments in any organisation. Any winning organisation's journey must respectfully review what is already in place by applying an open and extended communication process where people can listen, learn, challenge, test and importantly, accept where gaps may exist.

The communication process must be grounded by strategic objectives and the leadership must create an open environment for challenging and contributing to the thinking. An inclusive and engaging leader would clearly communicate the strategic goals, provide an overview of the pathway forward and humbly

invite the team to challenge theory, method and systems. The openness and pursuit of clarity minimises any 'who's right' behaviour and encourages a hunger to understand, use and improve the theory.

Example:

An organisation had a history of their decentralised site based leader groups being unable to agree to a corporate wide common approach to almost anything. It was a surprise when a 'community of practice' formed to discuss how to achieve commonality in the software products being used. They reached an agreement within three meetings.

How did this occur? By framing the community of practice with a clear strategic goal and respectfully allowing the site representatives appropriate discretion to find a pathway that suited their situation. Providing a common problem with a forward-looking context was unifying. Defining first what the corporate standard is and leaving each site to determine its own pathway to achieving the standard builds a high level of acceptance.

List of Essential Characteristics in WOM

Effective Leadership

1. Has a simple concise vision defines how the organisation creates value

2. Pursues clarity in communication with all employees and stakeholders

3. Engages at every level to ensure the organisation is on track to achieve its critical goals

4. Always seeks meaningful data to guide decision-making

5. Prioritises time to removing the barriers affecting the employees' ability to work to their full capability

6. Delegates authority to make control decisions to roles close to processes

7. Always seeks to delegate control and authority to roles close to the process

8. Pursues the simplification and improvement of systems

9. Actively encourages open, transparent and face-to-face communication

10. Positively demonstrates the six core values through their behaviour

11. Accepts role responsibility for improving the performance of the team

12. Develops standard work routines

13. Utilises planning processes based on valid data to determine the critical few priority actions

14. Assigns clear tasks and regularly reviews progress

15. Analyses variation in the execution of work compared with the plan

16. Has knowledge management systems that are owned by senior leadership to develop ASK-LEARN-SHARE behaviour throughout the organisation

Value Focus

Customer

17. Specifications for all products and services are clearly defined

18. The voice of the customer is incorporated into improvement processes via regular formal feedback processes

19. Market intelligence and competitor analysis is conducted that considers supply and demand, cost-effectiveness, quality and potential for substitution and business-changing innovation

Planning

20. A plan exists that defines how the organisation will ensure that the right people with the right skills are doing the right work in the right way to achieve the vision

21. The degree to which tasks are executed according to plan is measured and there is a focus on improvement

22. Planning estimates the level of risk (or confidence) in achieving a given performance output

23. Planning processes includes top-down and bottom-up verification processes to achieve alignment on the critical tasks required to achieve goals

24. No work can proceed without the approval of the budget owner

25. A financial model built upon process drivers is used to analyse and estimate the value of opportunities

26. The financial model considers the life expectancy of critical assets of the organisation

Analysing

27. A structured method is established to capture, analyse and improve ideas as input into planning

28. Process simulation is used to understand the impact of interactive variation and bottlenecks when considering high-cost interventions.

29. Discipline exists so ideas for improvement will be subjected to a valid cost/benefit analysis as part of determining priorities

Organisational Effectiveness

Learning

30. A 'way we work' program is delivered by leaders that communicates the vision, core values, work routines and role of leaders to employees

31. Communities of Practice (CoP) are used to build solutions that are owned within the organisation

Improving

32. Goals and objectives are prioritised based upon value

33. No more than five critical tasks are assigned to a person at a time

34. Employees have an expectation that they will be held accountable and be fairly rewarded for their work.

35. Individual performance assessment is always aligned to the overall performance of the team

36. The level of effectiveness in placing the right person in the right role at the right time is measured

37. Employee turnover is stable and at a rate less than 10% per year

38. All employees are engaged in seeking to minimise variation, including how work is planned and executed

Executing

39. The organisational design clearly describes how authority and resources are organised in order to achieve the vision

40. Levels of management do not exceed six, with a clear theory explaining the value of the work being done at each level

41. The number of direct reports fits within effective limits

42. All employees are given the authority and resources required to efficiently complete their standard work

43. All roles have defined: the purpose, authorities, accountabilities, skills, relationship to other roles (vertically and horizontally) and performance outputs

44. Customer relationship accountabilities are established in role descriptions

45. Standard jobs are approved within limits by the authorised person

46. Standard work routines for the organisation (including key communication and planning meetings) are established

47. Systems are defined, flowcharted and key roles and accountabilities allocated

Operational Excellence

Designing

48. SIPOC Model is understood and applied

49. Management of change is rigorously applied to ensure risk is managed to an acceptable level and improvement will be sustained

50. There is an investment in research and the application of leading technology in high-value opportunities

51. The organisation has access to the expertise required for designing experiments or undertaking complex projects

Measuring

52. Minimum output measures are run-charted and data guides decision-making

53. Process managers understand that control of variation at the input and in-process stages will lead to the least variation in outputs

54. Effective systems provide employees with the information needed

Controlling

55. It is understood that all variation is waste and it is the role of process managers to control variation within acceptable limits

56. Process managers utilise cause and effect maps to understand root causes

57. Whenever a process intervention is decided, the supporting theory is defined and captured

58. Process managers understand the impact of cumulative variations in processes

Example:

A large manufacturing organisation which sought to improve by implementing an excellence program identified significant gaps in effective leadership capability by applying WOM. Closing these gaps emerged as priority work before going further.

For each characteristic there was one of three current state outcomes:

no commitment to achieving the characteristic was evident

written supporting evidence that the characteristic exists

the characteristic is confirmed by people to be how the organisation works

Effective Leadership	Characterisitc	Current Capability
1	A simple concise vision defines how the organisation creates value.	capable
2	Pursues clarity in communication with all employees and stakeholders.	aligned
3	Engages at every level to ensure the organisation is on track to achieve its critical goals.	aligned
4	Always seeks meaningful data to guide decision making	aigned
5	Prioritises time to removing barriers affecting employee's ability to work to their full capability.	no evidence
6	Always seeks to delegate control and authority to act to roles close to the process.	no evidence
7	Pursues simplification and improvement to systems	no evidence
8	Actively encourages open, transparent and face-to-face communication	aligned
9	Positively demonstrates the six core values through their behaviour	aligned
10	Accepts role responsibility for improving the performance of the team	no evidence
11	Develops standard work routines	aligned
12	Utilises planning processes based on valid data to determine the critical few priority actions.	aligned
13	Assigns clear tasks and regularly reviewing progress	aligned
14	Analyses variation in execution of work compared to plan	no evidence
15	Knowledge management systems are owned by senior leadership to develop ASK-LEARN-SHARE behaviour throughout the organisation.	no evidence

Figure 24: Example of effective leadership diagnostic

In this case, the leaders were philosophically against the delegation of control to roles close to the process and did not accept the need for standard work routines.

Debate and visiting organisations where this was a confirmed characteristic were necessary before the leaders could see the value of them.

This same organisation was weak in analysing and executing characteristics. In this case, they made progress in addressing some of the gaps that improved performance. Just like a house plan provides a builder with a good idea of what must be built, so WOM provides the senior leadership (seeking to create

a best-in-class organisation) with the specification of what needs to be built.

Even if an organisation has not formed a clear objective of becoming best in class, WOM can be useful.

Example:

A volunteer organisation that had been established for decades recognised that membership was dwindling and ageing. The future of the organisation looked precarious. They needed to work out what they could do differently.

In this case, there was not a clear vision or perceived value in developing one. WOM helped the leaders realise why they needed a vision and how it could be used.

Imagine applying WOM in a coffee shop. All the capabilities are relevant even if the organisation has decided not to be the best coffee shop in its district. Even simply having a clear vision displayed in the café, standard tasks handwritten on flip cards, a customer feedback board asking for improvement suggestions stuck on a wall with a free coffee for the best suggestion of the week will help create a better performing coffee shop. The smaller the business, the easier it is to communicate and typically, the less complexity there is.

Concluding comments

Building a winning organisation is a journey and it takes time. An important determinant of success is constancy and focus of leadership. Whenever the senior leader changes there is always a high risk of 'change' or 're-branding'.

Building the key theory into the 'way we work' program is one way of ensuring a high degree of ownership at all levels. Clearly defined organisational design theory and effective people systems are also likely to help maintain consistency that will endure changes in senior leadership roles.

If the senior leadership has the authorities required and is likely to be in place for three years or more, there is a higher likelihood of success in pursuing a consistent approach to becoming a winning organisation. In larger organisations, it is always preferable for the most senior leader to own and drive the program. However, it is possible that discrete components of any organisation can independently progress. Without the most senior leader's ownership the discrete areas of progress are much more vulnerable.

The rate of progress in building a winning organisation is significantly impacted by the leadership's effectiveness and the complexity of the business. Significant progress can be achieved within nine months to three years and it is extremely important to measure whether progress is being made.

If there is no measurable progress within nine months, it is likely that there will be no progress within the next nine months and a review of the plan and the leadership is indicated. The implementation plan must deliver the strategic goals. The number of people trained, the number of projects completed or the dollar value delivered, can be a distraction and is probably not important.

Winning organisations are about delivering the strategic goals faster and with less. A global organisation recognised the outstanding performance of the shared services organisation due to the large amount of savings achieved. The organisation was a benchmark example of how shared services created value. The cost of a unit of production, however, had significantly increased during the same timeframe. There is a difference between reducing the cost of a service or consumable and reducing the cost of the product. Not focusing the shared service priorities on reducing the cost of the product was missing from the planning process. Reducing the cost of a service or component does not necessarily translate into a cost reduction for the product. Any service support group represents a silo that must be managed and where performance must be tied back to the production/delivery process output measures.

Without a focus on the critical few high-value tasks that determine resource allocation priorities and without the right feedback measures tracking performance, an organisation will be confused, wasteful and disillusioned.

The proposition of WOM is that there are certain essential characteristics that must exist for an organisation to confidently outperform the competition. These characteristics apply irrespective of its size. Leaders can assess their organisation for gaps using the set of characteristics, then with their people, determine how to close the most important gaps in a way that suits them.

Organisations require effective leadership that can engage and align the collective capability of the workforce to deliver what the customer wants. Effective leadership must behave in a manner that is consistently viewed positively against the core values.

Planning is required to ensure that the organisation can efficiently allocate scarce resources to the highest value opportunities.

Operational Excellence in safety—
My Personal Journey

I was fortunate to be given the role of managing the production team of the first aluminium smelter built in the Southern Hemisphere at a time where the technology was no longer contemporary. I was relatively young at the time and had contributed to several significant improvements in the efficiency of the operations within the process improvement department as a process engineer.

In this role, I was amazed at the gap between what was being done in the process compared with what the theory suggested. I was always inspired to solve a problem; even better, to achieve something that others thought was not possible.

The process itself relied on a significant degree of hard manual labour to keep it operating. In addition, there were significant environmental factors. Ambient temperature in some areas regularly exceeded 40 degrees Celsius and the radiant heat from the reduction cells could melt a hard hat if you spent too much time cleaning out lumps from molten baths operating at more than 1100 degrees. The culture was macho and the people who survived were typically tough characters.

People were being injured virtually every day. Sprains, strains, burns, asthma, falls, lacerations and broken bones were common. The culture of the company was one of continuous improvement, so as a young manager, I set about applying scientific thinking to analyse the data and address the root causes of the injuries.

Provided the injury trends were improving I thought I was doing my job. Every day I would review accident reports from the previous day with the management team and every day I would commit actions intended to prevent the recurrence. Many of the suggested solutions from frontline leaders were 'the employee needs to take more care' and I found this an unsatisfactory action from a root cause perspective.

Because the work was physically demanding, the selection criteria for new employees looked favourably on the candidates who were big and strong (playing Australian Rules Football, for example was an advantage). It was believed that the work was beyond the physical capability of women (this view was also supported by general practitioners advising on medical fitness requirements for the roles).

Upon reviewing the profiles of high performing personnel, I notice a few anomalies—some apparently very scrawny people were rated as high performers. This suggested that perhaps you did not need to be big and strong. I talked to these people and observed how they improvised to get the job done. Using brute strength was not an option for them.

Looking further at the data it became clearer that those who had brute strength often became injured by over-exerting themselves as they attempted to lift or push heavy loads.

My focus switched to the leadership and I began to enforce the use of methods that did not impose such heavy loads on one person. Hiring of physically fit, but not so strong people, including women for the first time, challenged conventional thinking. Improvements were achieved steadily and fewer strains and sprains resulted. Some new mechanised equipment was introduced, there was better personal protective equipment and improved control of the process itself helped reduced the need for extraordinarily physically demanding remedial actions.

While the rate of injuries dropped by a factor of four there were still injuries occurring on a weekly basis.

The NOSA five-star safety rating system was implemented, and after a time, the workplace looked much more organised, more colourful paint now demarcating areas and eventually we achieved a four-star NOSA rating level.

The injuries, while still improving, were still occurring regularly and it seemed that there were never-ending ways in which people could injure themselves. This was despite the team working long hours and being committed to making it better.

A new site general manager was appointed and one day attended one of my management meetings. He made it very clear that regardless of what we had been doing, the current safety performance was unacceptable and needed to change. It was a confronting and seemingly unkind response to all the hard work being done.

The concept of zero harm with the support of DuPont consultants was introduced. No longer was continuous improvement on safety acceptable, the operation must be managed without anyone getting hurt, EVER! This was confronting and at first seemed impossible. I had never imagined that it would be possible to eliminate all incidents from the current process.

The first step was to tell all the leaders that this was now the standard upon

which we would lead. If we could run without an incident for one day and then manage the hazards that could cause harm competently the next day and then the next, we could get there.

It was obvious that variation in what people were doing was the major factor to address. Proactive or what I called 'constructive paranoia' was required. This meant that everyone needed to run checklists of what could go wrong in their head or on paper and make sure that effective controls were in place before moving on to action.

As a symbol of my commitment I insisted on being immediately notified of every incident at any time. The operation ran 24/7 so I did not get much quality sleep for the next month.

Every time I managed to get to the scene of an incident within minutes of the event, I observed so much chaos, deviation from standard procedures and in some cases gross system deficiencies. The standard work of the leadership was grossly inadequate. The people were generally good people, they were simply not organised or focused well enough on the right things.

DuPont describes the need to create an interdependent culture where the whole team cares enough about the safety of others to look out for each other and have the courage and commitment to take interventions to ensure mistakes are corrected before any harm occurs. This made sense to me, given that in around 96% of incidents, the person injured, or someone nearby knew of a control action that could have prevented the incident.

People make mistakes, and sometimes those mistakes or shortcuts expose them to harmful energy exchanges. A simple probability analysis shows that two people are much less likely to make the same mistake at the same time. What if three people or all the people behaved that way? Put effective systems in place and the risk of mistakes drops right down.

The key was to create a culture where there was discipline, continuous improvement and a high care for the well-being of others to take the step to intervene if an unacceptable risk was perceived. My energy shifted from reviewing past events to building capability and desire within teams to address potentially harmful situations.

My biggest surprise was just how much improvement in safety was achieved by focusing on creating a culture of interdependence and fostering leaders that truly cared for the well-being of people. Leaders willingly felt and accepted accountability for every incident. This was a completely new paradigm.

Since that time, I have been fortunate to work with several organisations in different countries and cultures. I have learned more about the way the human brain operates and techniques that can improve the likelihood of leaders within organisations being successful in applying zero harm thinking to achieve excellence in safety. I have learned more about risk management and process safety systems for major hazardous facilities.

I have concluded that in most cases, leaders get the safety performance they deserve. When leaders truly care about the well-being of their people and are prepared to invest the right level of time and effort into safety they are rewarded.

If you do not get the result that you were expecting when following a theory, it can be because the theory was flawed or what was supposed to be done was not being done. I heard a term used in one organisation that was, 'We have lots of takeoffs around here but not many landings'. Many good theories, plans, systems, projects or intentions fail due to poor implementation.

So, if ensuring all hazards are identified and controlled within safe limits is the theory for how the organisation will operate then the leadership need to dedicate time to that work. A manager told me that he was no good at safety chats with people on the job. I asked him how many he had done. He said, 'five.' I said, 'Get to 100 and then we will talk again.' Like anything, people need to develop competence and that requires the 'doing' part.

In considering where effort in safety will achieve the greatest benefit, I believe in using the SIPOC Model. Focusing effort on control at the input and in-process stages is required to achieve the least variation at the output stage. A key safety process input is the time leaders devote to ensuring all hazards are controlled within safe limits.

The ideology of zero harm, when embraced, sets a different paradigm in terms of just how comprehensive and unwavering the focus must be in managing the risk from all potential hazards. Zero harm requires the organisation to establish layers of controls to prevent or limit individual mistakes from being able to cause damage. Reducing or eliminating variation and creating a culture where all employees are engaged in caring for their team mates and their processes is required.

There is evidence that people who believe they can influence their future by taking control are more likely to achieve their objectives than those who adopt a fatalistic viewpoint. Identifying hazards and effective ways to control them is not usually difficult.

The challenge is to turn these into habits, standard work routines, effective planning and discipline in work management. This will ensure there are enough checks and balances shared by enough people to prevent potentially harmful incidents.

References

Systems Leadership Creating Positive Organisations by Ian Macdonald, et al.

Requisite Organisation by Elliott Jacques.

Lean Thinking by James Womack and Daniel T Jones.

The Six Sigma Leader by Peter S Pande

Lean Six Sigma by Michael L George

The Goal by Eliyahu M.Goldratt

Seven Secrets of Great Entrepreneurial Masters by Allen E Fishman

MIT Sloan School of Business Vale Leadership Development Program

McKinsey Process Improvement Program

'Including 7s Model' by Robert H Waterman Jr and Tom Peters

MacAlear Consulting Asset Management Framework Materials

Sinclair and Associates

Riding the waves of culture by Peter B Smith, Shaun Dugan and Fons Trompenaars

Out of Crisis by Dr WE Deming

The Seven Habits of Highly Effective People by Steven Covey

Malandro Consulting Change Model

A Guide to Quality Control by Dr K Ishikawa

Royal Dutch Shell Ltd

Dupont Safety

www.ingramcontent.com/pod-product-compliance
Lightning Source LLC
Chambersburg PA
CBHW081807200326
41597CB00023B/4183